SERVSAFE®
MANAGER 6th EDITION BOOK

Updated with the
2013 FDA Food Code

ServSafe
National Restaurant Association

Disclaimer

Requests to use or reproduce material from this publication should be directed to:

Copyright Permissions
National Restaurant Association Solutions
175 West Jackson Boulevard, Suite 1500
Chicago, IL 60604-2814

Email: permissions@restaurant.org

Manager Book, ESX6R (with exam answer sheet)	ISBN	978-1-58280-310-4
Manager Book, ESV6R (with online exam voucher)	ISBN	978-1-58280-309-8
Manager Book, ES6R (text only)	ISBN	978-1-58280-308-1

Printed in the USA
10 9 8 7 6 5 4

Introduction

Chapter 1   Providing Safe Food

Chapter 2   Forms of Contamination

Chapter 3   The Safe Food Handler

Chapter 4   The Flow of Food: An Introduction

Chapter 5   The Flow of Food: Purchasing, Receiving, and Storage

A Message from
The National Restaurant Association

Congratulations! By opening this book, you are joining millions of foodservice professionals in taking the first step in a commitment to food safety. ServSafe® training helps you understand all of the food safety risks faced by your operation. Once you're aware of these risks, you can find ways to reduce them. This will help you keep your operation, your staff, and your customers safe.

Created by Foodservice Industry Leaders You can be confident knowing the ServSafe program was created by leaders in the foodservice industry. The topics you will learn in this book were determined by those who deal with the same food safety issues you face every day. From the basics of handwashing, to more complex topics such as foodborne pathogens, your industry peers have provided you with the building blocks to keep food safe throughout your operation.

Performed and Reinforced by You Food safety doesn't stop once you've completed your training and certification. It is now your responsibility to take the knowledge you learned and share it with your staff. When you return to your operation, start by answering the following questions to assess your food handler training:

- Do you have food safety training programs for both new and current staff?

- Do you have assessment tools to identify staff's food safety knowledge?

- Do you keep records documenting that staff have completed training?

About Your Certification To access your ServSafe Food Protection Manager Certification Exam results, register on ServSafe.com. You will need your class number, which your instructor will provide. Depending on how soon we receive your exam, results will be available approximately 10 business days after you take the exam. For security purposes, your exam results cannot be provided over the phone or sent through e-mail.

Your ServSafe Food Protection Manager Certification is valid for five years from your exam date. Local laws apply. Check with your local regulatory authority or company for specific recertification requirements.

If you have any questions about your certification or additional food handler training, please call (800) ServSafe (800.737.8723), or e-mail us at servicecenter@restaurant.org.

About the National Restaurant Association

The National Restaurant Association, founded in 1919, is the leading business association for the restaurant industry, which is comprised of 935,000 restaurant and foodservice outlets and a workforce of 12.8 million employees—making it the cornerstone of the economy, career opportunities, and community involvement. Along with the National Restaurant Association Educational Foundation, NRA Solutions and the Association work to represent, educate, and promote the rapidly growing industry. For more information, visit our Web site at restaurant.org.

Staying Connected with the National Restaurant Association throughout Your Career

The National Restaurant Association (NRA) has the resources and tools to support you throughout your education and career in the restaurant and foodservice industry. Through scholarships, educational programs, industry certifications, and member benefits, the NRA is your partner now and into the future.

- Scholarships: The NRA's philanthropic foundation, the National Restaurant Association Educational Foundation (NRAEF), offers scholarships to college students through its NRAEF Scholarship Program. These scholarships can help pave your way to an affordable higher education and may be applied to a culinary, restaurant management, or foodservice-related program at an accredited college or university. We encourage you to investigate the opportunities, which include access to special program scholarships for ProStart students who earn the National Certificate of Achievement, as well as ManageFirst Program® students. You may be awarded one NRAEF scholarship per calendar year—make sure you keep applying every year! The NRAEF partners with state restaurant associations to offer student scholarships. Check with your state to see if they offer additional scholarship opportunities. The NRAEF also offers professional development scholarships for educators. Visit nraef.org/scholarships for information.

- College education: As you research and apply to colleges and universities to continue your industry education, look for schools offering the NRA's **ManageFirst Program**. Just like *Foundations of Restaurant Management & Culinary Arts*, the ManageFirst Program and curriculum materials were developed with input from the restaurant and foodservice industry and academic partners. This management program teaches you practical skills needed to face real-world challenges in the industry, including interpersonal communication, ethics, accounting skills, and more. The program includes the ten topics listed below, plus ServSafe Food Safety and ServSafe Alcohol®:

  - Controlling Foodservice Costs
  - Hospitality and Restaurant Management
  - Hospitality Human Resources Management and Supervision
  - Customer Service
  - Principles of Food and Beverage Management
  - Purchasing
  - Hospitality Accounting
  - Bar and Beverage Management
  - Nutrition
  - Hospitality and Restaurant Marketing

You can also earn the ManageFirst Professional® (MFP™) credential by passing five required ManageFirst exams and completing 800 work hours in the industry. Having the MFP on your resume tells employers that you have the management skills needed to succeed in the industry. To learn more about ManageFirst or to locate ManageFirst schools, visit managefirst.restaurant.org.

- Certification: In the competitive restaurant field, industry certifications can help you stand out among a crowd of applicants.

  The NRA's **ServSafe** Food Protection Manager Certification is nationally recognized. Earning your certification tells the industry that you know food safety and the critical importance of its role—and enables you to share food safety knowledge with every other employee.

  Through ServSafe Food Safety, you'll master sanitation, the flow of food through an operation, sanitary facilities, and pest management. ServSafe is the training that is learned, remembered, shared, and used. And that makes it the strongest food safety training choice for you. For more information on ServSafe, visit ServSafe.com.

  The challenges surrounding alcohol service in restaurants have increased dramatically. To prepare you to address these challenges, the NRA offers **ServSafe Alcohol**. As you continue to work in the industry, responsible alcohol service is an issue that will touch your business, your customers, and your community. Armed with your ServSafe Alcohol Certificate, you can make an immediate impact on an establishment. Through the program, you'll learn essential responsible alcohol service information, including alcohol laws and responsibilities, evaluating intoxication levels, dealing with difficult situations, and checking identification. Please visit ServSafe.com/alcohol to learn more about ServSafe Alcohol.

- National Restaurant Association membership: As you move into the industry, seek out careers in restaurants that are **members of the NRA and your state restaurant association.** Encourage any operation you are part of to join the national and state organizations. During your student years, the NRA also offers student memberships that give you access to industry research and information that can be an invaluable resource. For more information, or to join as a student member, visit restaurant.org.

- Management credentials: After you've established yourself in the industry, strive for the industry's highest management certification—the NRA's **Foodservice Management Professional**® (FMP®). The FMP certification recognizes exceptional managers and supervisors who have achieved the highest level of knowledge, experience, and professionalism that is most valued by our industry. You become eligible to apply and sit for the FMP exam after you've worked as a supervisor in the industry for three years. Passing the FMP exam places you in select company; you will have joined the ranks of leading industry professionals. The FMP certification is also an impressive credential to add to your title and resume. For more information on the Foodservice Management Professional certification, visit managefirst.restaurant.org.

Make the NRA your partner throughout your education and career. Take advantage of the NRA's scholarship, training, certification, and membership benefits that will launch you into your career of choice. Together we will lead this industry into an even brighter future.

Acknowledgements

The development of the *ServSafe Manager Book* would not have been possible without the expertise of our many advisors and manuscript reviewers. Thank you to the following people and organizations for their time, effort, and dedication to creating this sixth edition.

Curt Archambault, Jack In The Box

Petra Balli, ARAMARK

Kelly Blakely, Valero

Robert Brown, Whole Foods

Nancy Caldarola, Concept Associates Inc.

Don Culver, Army and Air Force Exchange Service

Ana De La Torre, Santa Paula Oil Corp. dba To Go Stores

Claudia Diez, University of Minnesota

Jeff Drozdowski, Little Caesars

Shannon Flynn, Potbelly Sandwich Works

Kendra Kauppi, University of Minnesota

Linda Kender, Johnson & Wales University

Mahmood Khan, Virginia Tech

Geoff Luebkemann, Florida Restaurant and Lodging Association

Dave McNinch, Washoe County District Health Department

Mark Miklos, Waffle House

Eric Moore, ARAMARK

Michael Pozit, Integrated Food Service Consulting Corp.

Angela Sanchez, CKE Restaurants

Victoria Sánchez Martínez, New Mexico Restaurant Association

Mary L Sandford, Burger King Corporation

Edward Sherwin, Sherwin Food Safety

Allison Straley, WESCO, Inc.

Alan Tart, U.S. Food and Drug Administration

Cameron Underwood, Valero

Wanda Vinson, Long John Silver's

Justin Waldrep, RaceTrac

Brian Wickman, Compass Group North America

Boskovich Farms, Inc.

Centers for Disease Control and Prevention

Le Cordon Bleu College of Culinary Arts Chicago

How to Use the *ServSafe Manager Book*

The plan below will help you study and remember the food safety principles in this book.

At the Beginning of Each Chapter

Before you start reading each chapter, you can prepare by reviewing these sections.

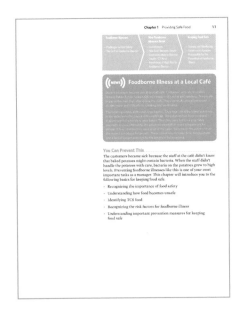

Advanced Organizer   Chapter content is divided into sections. Each section begins with a graphic organizer at the top of the page. The graphic organizer identifies each section within that chapter. The darker blue color indicates where you are in the chapter structure.

The key topics for each section are also displayed. You will always know what to expect within a section.

In the News   This real-world story introduces you to the chapter. It shows you how not practicing food safety can negatively impact an operation. What happens in the story relates to the concepts you will learn in the chapter.

You Can Prevent This   This section tells you the negative things that happened in the "In the News" story and how the situation could have been prevented. Additionally, it lists what you will learn in the chapter. These topics are the essential practices for keeping food in your operation safe.

Throughout Each Chapter

Use the following learning tools to help you identify and learn key food safety principles as you read each chapter.

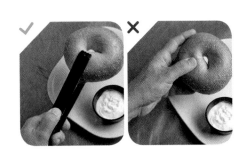

Photos   Photos give you visual examples of key principles in the book. They are either in the margin next to a principle or in the text itself. Some of the photos show you what you should do, while others show you what you shouldn't do. If the photo is a positive practice, it has a ✔ in the left corner. If the photo is a negative practice, it has a ✘ in the left corner, meaning that this practice should never be done.

Charts, illustrations, and tables   These visuals either present or organize content so that it is easier for you to learn. In some instances, they are used to reinforce key principles in the book.

Pathogen alert icons   These icons point to pathogens within the text and the actions that you can take to prevent a specific pathogen from making people sick.

Within Each Chapter

Apply Your Knowledge activities   These activities allow you to apply the key food safety practices in a chapter. At the end of each major topic, you can practice what you learned. Answers are at the end of each chapter.

Something to Think About...   Many food safety stories appear in this book. Some of these real-world stories focus on foodborne illnesses that happened because food was not handled correctly. They show the importance of following food safety practices. They also allow you to apply what you have learned by asking how the illness could have been prevented. Other stories show you real-world solutions to food safety problems that operations have experienced. These solutions can help you improve the food safety practices in your own operation.

How This Relates to Me   Some of the food safety practices in this book may differ from your local laws. To help you remember these differences, you can record your local regulatory requirements in these write-in areas of the book.

At the End of Each Chapter

The end of each chapter gives you three opportunities to review the content you just learned.

Chapter summary   A bulleted summary is at the end of each chapter to help remind you of the major topics you learned.

Chapter review case studies   These food safety case studies ask you to identify the errors made by the food handlers in each story, and the practices that the staff should have followed.

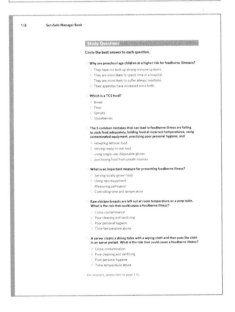

Study questions   These multiple-choice questions are based on key food safety principles. If you have trouble answering them, you should review the content again. Answers are at the end of each chapter.

chapter 1
Providing Safe Food

Foodborne Illnesses	How Foodborne Illnesses Occur	Keeping Food Safe
— Challenges to Food Safety — The Cost of Foodborne Illnesses	— Contaminants — How Food Becomes Unsafe — Food Most Likely to Become Unsafe: TCS Food — Populations at High Risk for Foodborne Illnesses	— Training and Monitoring — Government Agencies Responsible for the Prevention of Foodborne Illness

((NEWS)) Foodborne Illness at a Local Café

Dozens of people became sick at a small café. Customers who ate the cafe's famous Baked Potato Salad called to complain of nausea and vomiting. These calls began within two days after eating the dish. They eventually also experienced double vision and difficulty in speaking and swallowing.

The local regulatory authorities investigated. They found that the baked potatoes in the salad were the source of the outbreak. The potatoes had been wrapped in aluminum foil when they were baked. Then they were left on a prep table overnight to cool. Ultimately, the potatoes were left at room temperature for almost 18 hours before they were used in the salad. Bacteria on the potatoes had the correct conditions for growth. These conditions included time, temperature, and a lack of oxygen provided by the potatoes' foil wrapping.

You Can Prevent This

The customers became sick because the staff at the café didn't know that baked potatoes might contain bacteria. When the staff didn't handle the potatoes with care, bacteria on the potatoes grew to high levels. Preventing foodborne illnesses like this is one of your most important tasks as a manager. This chapter will introduce you to the following basics for keeping food safe.

- Recognizing the importance of food safety
- Understanding how food becomes unsafe
- Identifying TCS food
- Recognizing the risk factors for foodborne illness
- Understanding important prevention measures for keeping food safe

Foodborne Illnesses	How Foodborne Illnesses Occur	Keeping Food Safe
— Challenges to Food Safety — The Cost of Foodborne Illnesses	— Contaminants — How Food Becomes Unsafe — Food Most Likely to Become Unsafe: TCS Food — Populations at High Risk for Foodborne Illnesses	— Training and Monitoring — Government Agencies Responsible for the Prevention of Foodborne Illness

Foodborne Illnesses

Being a foodservice manager isn't easy. You have responsibilities to your operation, to your staff, and to your customers. The best way to meet those responsibilities is to keep the food you serve safe. To start, you must learn what foodborne illnesses are and the challenges you will face in preventing them. You simply can't afford not to. The costs of a foodborne-illness outbreak can be devastating.

Challenges to Food Safety

A foodborne illness is a disease transmitted to people by food. An illness is considered an outbreak when:

- Two or more people have the same symptoms after eating the same food.

- An investigation is conducted by state and local regulatory authorities.

- The outbreak is confirmed by a laboratory analysis.

Each year, millions of people get sick from unsafe food.

Foodservice operations work hard to minimize foodborne illnesses. As a result of these efforts, foodborne illnesses have declined in recent years. However, operations still face many challenges to food safety.

Time   Pressure to work quickly can make it hard to take the time to follow food safety practices.

Language and culture   Your staff may speak a different language than you do. This can make it difficult to communicate. Cultural differences can also influence how food handlers view food safety.

Literacy and education   Staff often have different levels of education. This makes it more challenging to teach them food safety.

Pathogens   Illness-causing microorganisms are more frequently found on types of food that once were considered safe.

Unapproved suppliers   Food that is received from suppliers that are not practicing food safety can cause a foodborne-illness outbreak.

High-risk customers   The number of customers at high risk for getting a foodborne illness is increasing. An example of this is the growing elderly population.

Staff turnover   Training new staff leaves less time for food safety training.

The ServSafe program will provide you with the tools you need to overcome the challenges in managing a good food safety program.

The Cost of Foodborne Illnesses

Foodborne illnesses cost the United States billions of dollars each year. National Restaurant Association figures show that one foodborne-illness outbreak can cost an operation thousands of dollars. It can even result in closure.

Costs of a Foodborne Illness to an Operation

 Loss of customers and sales

 Loss of reputation

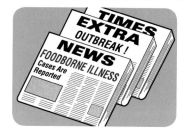 Negative media exposure

 Lowered staff morale

 Lawsuits and legal fees

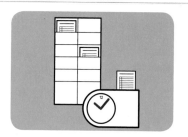 Staff missing work

 Increased insurance premiums

 Staff retraining

Most important are the human costs. Victims of foodborne illnesses may experience the following.

- Lost work

- Medical costs and long-term disability

- Death

Foodborne Illnesses	How Foodborne Illnesses Occur	Keeping Food Safe
— Challenges to Food Safety — The Cost of Foodborne Illnesses	— Contaminants — How Food Becomes Unsafe — Food Most Likely to Become Unsafe: TCS Food — Populations at High Risk for Foodborne Illnesses	— Training and Monitoring — Government Agencies Responsible for the Prevention of Foodborne Illness

How Foodborne Illnesses Occur

Unsafe food is usually the result of contamination, which is the presence of harmful substances in food. To prevent foodborne illnesses, you must recognize the contaminants that can make food unsafe. These can come from pathogens, chemicals, or physical objects. They might also come from certain unsafe practices in your operation.

Contaminants

Contaminants are divided into three categories.

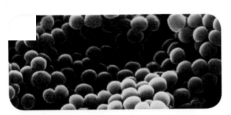

Biological   Pathogens are the greatest threat to food safety. They include certain viruses, parasites, fungi, and bacteria, as shown in the photo at left. Some plants, mushrooms, and seafood that carry harmful toxins (poisons) are also included in this group.

Chemical   Foodservice chemicals can contaminate food if they are used incorrectly. The photo at left shows one example of how chemicals may contaminate food. Chemical contaminants can include cleaners, sanitizers, and polishes.

Physical   Foreign objects such as metal shavings, staples, and bandages can get into food. So can glass, dirt, and even bag ties. The photo at left shows this type of physical contaminant. Naturally occurring objects, such as fish bones in fillets, are another example.

Each of the contaminants listed above is a danger to food safety. But biological contaminants are responsible for most foodborne illness.

How Food Becomes Unsafe

If food handlers do not handle food correctly, it can become unsafe. These are the five most common food-handling mistakes, or risk factors, that can cause a foodborne illness.

1. Purchasing food from unsafe sources
2. Failing to cook food correctly
3. Holding food at incorrect temperatures
4. Using contaminated equipment
5. Practicing poor personal hygiene

Except for purchasing food from unsafe sources, each mistake listed above is related to four main factors. These include time-temperature abuse, cross-contamination, poor personal hygiene, and poor cleaning and sanitizing.

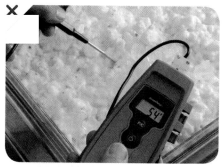

Time-temperature abuse Food has been time-temperature abused when it has stayed too long at temperatures that are good for the growth of pathogens. A foodborne illness can result if food is time-temperature abused. This can happen in many ways.

- Food is not held or stored at the correct temperature, as shown in the photo at left.
- Food is not cooked or reheated enough to kill pathogens.
- Food is not cooled correctly.

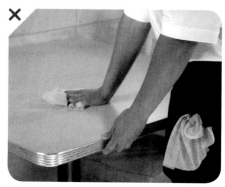

Cross-contamination Pathogens can be transferred from one surface or food to another. This is called cross-contamination. It can cause a foodborne illness in many ways.

- Contaminated ingredients are added to food that receives no further cooking.
- Ready-to-eat food touches contaminated surfaces.
- Contaminated food touches or drips fluids onto cooked or ready-to-eat food, as shown in the photo at left.
- A food handler touches contaminated food and then touches ready-to-eat food.
- Contaminated cleaning cloths touch food-contact surfaces.

Poor personal hygiene Food handlers can cause a foodborne illness if they do any of the following actions.

- Fail to wash their hands correctly after using the restroom.
- Cough or sneeze on food.
- Touch or scratch wounds and then touch food, as shown in the photo at left.
- Work while sick.

Poor cleaning and sanitizing Pathogens can be spread to food if equipment has not been cleaned and sanitized correctly between uses. This can happen in the following ways.

- Equipment and utensils are not washed, rinsed, and sanitized between uses.
- Food-contact surfaces are wiped clean rather than being washed, rinsed, and sanitized.
- Wiping cloths are not stored in a sanitizer solution between uses, as shown in the photo at left.
- Sanitizing solutions are not at the required levels to sanitize objects.

Food Most Likely to Become Unsafe: TCS Food

Pathogens grow well in the food pictured below. It needs time and temperature control to limit this growth. For this reason, this food is called TCS food—food requiring time and temperature control for safety.

 • Milk and dairy products

 • Shell eggs (except those treated to eliminate nontyphoidal *Salmonella*)

 • Meat: beef, pork, and lamb

 • Poultry

 • Fish

 • Shellfish and crustaceans

 • Baked potatoes

 • Heat-treated plant food, such as cooked rice, beans, and vegetables

 • Tofu or other soy protein
• Synthetic ingredients, such as textured soy protein in meat alternatives

 • Sprouts and sprout seeds

 • Sliced melons
• Cut tomatoes
• Cut leafy greens

 • Untreated garlic-and-oil mixtures

Like TCS food, ready-to-eat food also needs careful handling to prevent contamination. Ready-to-eat food is exactly what it sounds like: food that can be eaten without further preparation, washing, or cooking. Ready-to-eat food includes cooked food, washed fruit and vegetables (whole and cut), and deli meat. Bakery items and sugar, spices, and seasonings are also included.

Populations at High Risk for Foodborne Illnesses

Certain groups of people have a higher risk of getting a foodborne illness.

Elderly people

People's immune systems weaken with age. The immune system is the body's defense against illness.

Preschool-age children

Very young children have not built up strong immune systems.

People with compromised immune systems

- People with cancer or on chemotherapy
- People with HIV/AIDS
- Transplant recipients
- People taking certain medications

Apply Your Knowledge

What's the Cause?

Write an ✖ next to the 5 most common causes of foodborne illness.

① _____ Purchasing food from unsafe sources

② _____ Allowing pests to enter the operation

③ _____ Failing to cook food correctly

④ _____ Failing to rotate food during storage

⑤ _____ Using contaminated equipment

⑥ _____ Holding food at incorrect temperatures

⑦ _____ Practicing poor personal hygiene

⑧ _____ Failing to store dry food correctly

Which Is It?

Write an ✖ next to the food that needs time and temperature control to keep it safe.

① _____ Chopped lettuce

② _____ Sliced watermelon

③ _____ Dry rice

④ _____ Flour

⑤ _____ Cooked carrots

⑥ _____ Cheese

For answers, please turn to page 1.13.

Foodborne Illnesses	How Foodborne Illnesses Occur	Keeping Food Safe
— Challenges to Food Safety — The Cost of Foodborne Illnesses	— Contaminants — How Food Becomes Unsafe — Food Most Likely to Become Unsafe: TCS Food — Populations at High Risk for Foodborne Illnesses	— Training and Monitoring — Government Agencies Responsible for the Prevention of Foodborne Illness

Keeping Food Safe

Now that you know how food can become unsafe, you can use this knowledge to keep food safe. Focus on these measures.

- Controlling time and temperature

- Preventing cross-contamination

- Practicing personal hygiene

- Purchasing from approved, reputable suppliers

- Cleaning and sanitizing

Set up standard operating procedures that focus on these areas. The ServSafe program will show you how to design these procedures in later chapters.

Training and Monitoring

As a manager, your job is more than just understanding food safety practices and creating the necessary procedures. You also must train your staff to follow these procedures, as shown in the photo at left. Staff should be trained when they are first hired and on an ongoing basis. Your entire staff needs general food safety knowledge. Other knowledge will be specific to the tasks performed on the job. For example, everyone needs to know the correct way to wash their hands. However, only receiving staff needs to know how to inspect produce during receiving.

Staff need to be retrained in food safety regularly. When a food handler completes this training, document it. Once staff are trained, monitor them to make sure they are following procedures.

Government Agencies Responsible for the Prevention of Foodborne Illness

Several government agencies take leading roles in the prevention of foodborne illness in the United States. The Food and Drug Administration (FDA) and the U.S. Department of Agriculture (USDA) inspect food and perform other critical duties. State and local regulatory authorities create regulations and inspect operations. Agencies such as the Centers for Disease Control and Prevention (CDC) and the U. S. Public Health Service (PHS) help as well.

The Role of the FDA

The FDA inspects all food except meat, poultry, and eggs. The agency also regulates food transported across state lines. In addition, the FDA issues a *Food Code.* This science-based code provides recommendations for food safety regulations. The *Food Code* was created for city, county, state, and tribal agencies. These agencies regulate foodservice for the following groups.

- Restaurants and retail food stores
- Vending operations
- Schools and day care centers
- Hospitals and nursing homes

Although the FDA recommends that states adopt the *Food Code,* it cannot require it. The FDA also provides technical support and training. This is available for industry and regulatory agencies.

Other Agencies

Several other agencies have an important role in food safety and the prevention of foodborne illness.

USDA   The U.S. Department of Agriculture regulates and inspects meat, poultry, and eggs. The USDA also regulates food that crosses state boundaries or involves more than one state.

CDC and PHS   These agencies assist the FDA, USDA, and state and local health departments. They conduct research into the causes of foodborne-illness outbreaks. They also assist in investigating outbreaks.

State and local regulatory authorities   Regulatory authorities write or adopt code that regulates retail and foodservice operations. Codes may differ from the *FDA Food Code,* because these agencies are not required to adopt it.

Regulatory authorities have many responsibilities. Here are some of the responsibilities related to food safety.

- Inspecting operations
- Enforcing regulations
- Investigating complaints and illnesses
- Issuing licenses and permits
- Approving construction
- Reviewing and approving HACCP plans

Apply Your Knowledge

Who Does What?

Write the letter of the government agency in the space provided. Some letters may be used more than once.

Ⓐ FDA

Ⓑ USDA

Ⓒ CDC and PHS

Ⓓ State and local
   health departments

① _____ Writes the codes that regulate retail and foodservice operations

② _____ Conducts research into the causes of foodborne-illness outbreaks

③ _____ Inspects meat, poultry, and eggs

④ _____ Writes the *Food Code*

⑤ _____ Inspects retail and foodservice operations

For answers, please turn to page 1.13.

Chapter Summary

- As a foodservice manager, you have responsibilities to your operation, staff, and customers. The best way to meet those responsibilities is to keep the food you serve safe.

- A foodborne illness is a disease transmitted to people by food. An illness is considered an outbreak when two or more people have the same symptoms after eating the same food.

- Three types of contaminants threaten food safety. They are: biological, chemical, and physical. Of these, biological contaminants, such as pathogens, pose the greatest danger.

- Food handlers who do not follow the correct procedures can also threaten the safety of food. They can do this when they fail to cook food enough and when they hold it at incorrect temperatures. Food handlers can also cause an illness when they use contaminated equipment and when they practice poor personal hygiene.

- Food has been time-temperature abused when it has stayed too long at temperatures that are good for the growth of pathogens. Pathogens can be transferred from one surface or food to another. This is called cross-contamination. Pathogens can also be spread to food if equipment has not been cleaned and sanitized correctly between uses.

- Pathogens grow well in TCS food. To prevent this growth, this food needs time and temperature control.

- Some groups are at a higher risk of getting sick from unsafe food. They include preschool-age children; the elderly; people with cancer or on chemotherapy; people with HIV/AIDS; transplant recipients; and people on certain medications.

- Important prevention measures for keeping food safe are: controlling time and temperature; preventing cross-contamination; practicing good personal hygiene; purchasing from approved, reputable suppliers; and cleaning and sanitizing items correctly.

Chapter Review Case Study

Food safety is important to every foodservice operation, and the costs of a foodborne-illness outbreak can be high. However, you can avoid outbreaks by recognizing the importance of food safety; recognizing how food can become unsafe; identifying the risks associated with high-risk populations; training and monitoring staff; and following the keys to food safety.

Now, take what you have learned in this chapter and apply it to the following case study.

Jerry was not happy because he was working by himself. His coworker had called in sick and they were expecting their regular Wednesday night group of softball players. Jerry was not feeling too well himself, and on top of this, the large group canceled at the last minute. Unfortunately, Jerry had already started cooking a dozen burgers on the grill.

Jerry finished cooking the hamburger patties until they were well-done, and then he put them in a pan on the counter. "Maybe someone will order a burger later," he thought. Because there were no customers yet, he made a quick run to the restroom. When he finished, he wiped his hands on his apron, combed his hair, and headed back to the kitchen.

Twenty minutes later, Jerry got his first customers of the evening. They were an elderly man and his four-year-old granddaughter. Jerry was happy when they ordered a burger to share. "Cook it medium," the man said. It looked like the premade burgers would stay on the counter for a while.

Jerry went back to the kitchen and put a fresh patty on the grill. Then he wiped off the cutting board he had used earlier for prepping raw chicken. He sliced the tomatoes and onion. When the burger just passed medium-rare, he plated it up.

When Jerry delivered the food, the little girl asked for a glass of water. Jerry grabbed a glass and used it to scoop some ice. But, the glass broke. Jerry carefully picked the broken glass out of the ice machine. Then he got the girl a fresh glass for the ice water.

① What did Jerry do wrong?

_____

_____

_____

② What should Jerry have done?

_____

_____

_____

For answers, please turn to page 1.13.

Study Questions

Circle the best answer to each question.

① **Why are preschool-age children at a higher risk for foodborne illnesses?**

  A They have not built up strong immune systems.

  B They are more likely to spend time in a hospital.

  C They are more likely to suffer allergic reactions.

  D Their appetites have increased since birth.

② **Which is a TCS food?**

  A Bread

  B Flour

  C Sprouts

  D Strawberries

③ **The 5 common mistakes that can lead to foodborne illness are failing to cook food adequately, holding food at incorrect temperatures, using contaminated equipment, practicing poor personal hygiene, and**

  A reheating leftover food.

  B serving ready-to-eat food.

  C using single-use, disposable gloves.

  D purchasing food from unsafe sources.

④ **What is an important measure for preventing foodborne illness?**

  A Serving locally grown food

  B Using new equipment

  C Measuring pathogens

  D Controlling time and temperature

⑤ **Raw chicken breasts are left out at room temperature on a prep table. What is the risk that could cause a foodborne illness?**

  A Cross-contamination

  B Poor cleaning and sanitizing

  C Poor personal hygiene

  D Time-temperature abuse

⑥ **A server cleans a dining table with a wiping cloth and then puts the cloth in an apron pocket. What is the risk that could cause a foodborne illness?**

  A Cross-contamination

  B Poor cleaning and sanitizing

  C Poor personal hygiene

  D Time-temperature abuse

For answers, please turn to page 1.13.

Answers

1.7   What's the Cause?

1, 3, 5, 6, and 7 should be marked.

1.7   Which Is It?

1, 2, 5, and 6 should be marked.

1.10   Who Does What?

① D   ④ A

② C   ⑤ D

③ B

1.11   Chapter Review Case Study

① Here is what Jerry did wrong.

- He came into work sick.

- He left cooked burgers sitting out at room temperature. This is time-temperature abuse.

- He wore his apron into the restroom. He also didn't wash his hands after using the restroom and wiped his hands on his apron. This is poor personal hygiene.

- He sliced tomatoes on a cutting board that had been used for chicken. This is cross-contamination.

- He scooped ice with a glass. The broken glass in the ice machine is a physical hazard.

- While scooping the ice, Jerry's hand could have touched the ice, leading to cross-contamination of the ice.

② Here is what Jerry should have done.

- He should have called in sick. If Jerry was feeling ill, there's a chance he could have made his customers sick.

- When he realized he had made too many hamburger patties, he should have either stored the burgers in hot-holding, or thrown them out.

- He should have washed his hands after using the bathroom and after touching his hair. He should have removed his apron before using the restroom.

- When slicing the tomatoes, Jerry should have first washed, rinsed, and sanitized the cutting board. Also, he could have used a separate cutting board.

- He should have used the correct scoop for the ice.

1.12   Study Questions

① A   ④ D

② C   ⑤ D

③ D   ⑥ B

chapter 2
Forms of Contamination

((NEWS)) *Shigella* Outbreak

Sixteen guests and three catering hall staff got sick with *Shigella* spp. The guests were part of a large group of National Guard veterans at a reunion. They ate at a large and popular catering hall located in the southeastern United States.

Within one to three days after the catered event, reports began to come into the local regulatory authority. Those who had gotten sick reported very similar symptoms. Each had experienced stomach cramps, fever, and diarrhea. Three people went to the emergency room to seek treatment.

The specific food involved was never determined. But the regulatory authority confirmed that the outbreak was likely caused by the catering hall's lead cook. He was not feeling well the morning of the luncheon when he reported to work. He also had failed to wash his hands many times during his morning shift. The cook had prepped the food that was served at the luncheon.

The catering hall's owners and management team worked with the local regulatory authority to change procedures about staff illnesses. They also started an aggressive training program that focused on correct handwashing.

You Can Prevent This

Illnesses such as the one in the story above can be prevented if you understand how pathogens contaminate food. In this chapter, you will learn about the following topics.

- Biological, chemical, and physical contaminants and how to prevent them

- How to prevent the deliberate contamination of food

- How to respond to a foodborne-illness outbreak

- Common food allergens and how to prevent reactions to them

Biological, Chemical, and Physical Contaminants		Deliberate Contamination of Food	Responding to a Foodborne-Illness Outbreak	Food Allergens
— How Contamination Happens — Biological Contamination — Symptoms of Foodborne Illness — Bacteria	— Viruses — Parasites — Fungi — Biological Toxins — Chemical Contaminants — Physical Contaminants			— Allergy Symptoms — Common Food Allergens — Preventing Allergic Reactions

Biological, Chemical, and Physical Contaminants

One of the foodservice manager's most important roles is to prevent any type of contamination of food from occurring. Contamination is the presence of harmful substances in food. Those substances can be biological, chemical, or physical. Most contaminants cause foodborne illness. Others can result in physical injury.

How Contamination Happens

Contaminants come from a variety of places. Many contaminants are found in the animals we use for food. Others come from the air, contaminated water, and dirt. Some contaminants occur naturally in food, such as the bones in fish.

Food can be contaminated on purpose. But most food contamination happens accidentally. Most contaminants get into food and onto food-contact surfaces because of the way that people handle them. For example, food handlers who don't wash their hands after using the restroom may contaminate food and surfaces with feces from their fingers. Once the food that the food handler touched is eaten, a foodborne illness may result. This is called the fecal-oral route of contamination.

Food handlers can also pass on contaminants when they are in contact with a person who is ill. Some contaminants are passed very easily in any of these ways.

- From person to person
- Through sneezing or vomiting onto food or food-contact surfaces
- From touching dirty food-contact surfaces and equipment, and then touching food

Simple mistakes can result in contamination. For example, allowing ready-to-eat food to touch surfaces that have come in contact with raw meat, seafood, and poultry can lead to contamination. An example is shown in the photo at left. Storing food incorrectly or cleaning produce incorrectly can also lead to contamination. So can the failure to spot signs of pests in the establishment, because pests are a major source of disease.

Biological Contamination

Microorganisms are small, living organisms that can be seen only through a microscope. Many microorganisms are harmless, but some can cause illness. Harmful microorganisms are called pathogens. Some pathogens make you sick when you eat them. Others produce poisons—or toxins—that make you sick.

Understanding these biological contaminants is the first step to preventing foodborne-illness outbreaks. There are four types of pathogens that can contaminate food and cause foodborne illness. These are bacteria, viruses, parasites, and fungi (which includes molds and yeast).

According to the Food and Drug Administration (FDA), there are over 40 different kinds of bacteria, viruses, parasites, and molds that can occur in food and cause a foodborne illness. Of these, six have been singled out by the FDA. These have been dubbed the Big Six because they are highly contagious and can cause severe illness. The Big Six include the following.

- *Shigella* spp.
- *Salmonella* Typhi
- Nontyphoidal *Salmonella* (NTS)
- Shiga toxin-producing *Escherichia coli* (STEC), also known as *E. coli*
- Hepatitis A
- Norovirus

Symptoms of Foodborne Illness

The symptoms of a foodborne illness vary, depending on which illness a person has. But most victims of foodborne illness share some common symptoms.

- Diarrhea
- Vomiting
- Fever
- Nausea
- Abdominal cramps
- Jaundice (a yellowing of the skin and eyes)

Not every person who is sick with a foodborne illness will have all of these symptoms. Nor are the symptoms of a foodborne illness limited to this list.

How quickly foodborne-illness symptoms appear in a person is known as the onset time of the illness. Onset times depend on the type of foodborne illness a person has. They can range from 30 minutes to as long as six weeks. How severe the illness is can also vary, from mild diarrhea to death.

Bacteria

Bacteria that cause foodborne illness have some basic characteristics.

Location   Bacteria can be found almost everywhere. They live in and on our bodies. Some types of bacteria keep us healthy, while others cause illness.

Detection   Bacteria cannot be seen, smelled, or tasted.

Growth   If FAT TOM conditions are correct, bacteria will grow in rapid numbers.

Prevention   The most important way to prevent bacteria from causing a foodborne illness is to control time and temperature.

What Bacteria Need to Grow

Bacteria need six conditions to grow. You can remember these conditions by thinking of the words FAT TOM.

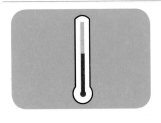

Food   Most bacteria need nutrients to survive. TCS food supports the growth of bacteria better than other types of food.

Time   Bacteria need time to grow. The more time bacteria spend in the temperature danger zone, the more opportunity they have to grow to unsafe levels.

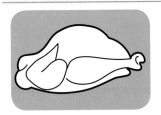

Acidity   Bacteria grow best in food that contains little or no acid. pH is the measure of acidity. The pH scale ranges from 0 to 14.0. A value of 0 is highly acidic, while a value of 14 is highly alkaline. A pH of 7 is neutral. Bacteria grows best in food that is neutral to slightly acidic.

Oxygen   Some bacteria need oxygen to grow. Others grow when oxygen is not there.

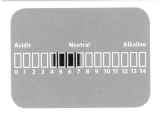

Temperature   Bacteria grow rapidly between 41°F and 135°F (5°C and 57°C). This range is known as the temperature danger zone. Bacteria grow even more rapidly from 70°F to 125°F (21°C to 52°C). Bacteria growth is limited when food is held above or below the temperature danger zone.

Moisture   Bacteria grow well in food with high levels of moisture. The amount of moisture available in food for this growth is called water activity (a_w). The a_w scale ranges from 0.0 to 1.0. The higher the value, the more available moisture in the food. For example, water has a water activity of 1.0.

You can help keep food safe by controlling FAT TOM. In your operation, however, you will most likely be able to control only time and temperature. To control temperature, you must do your best to keep TCS food out of the temperature danger zone. To control time, you must limit how long food spends in the temperature danger zone.

Major Bacteria that Cause Foodborne Illness

Many types of bacteria can cause a foodborne illness. The FDA has identified four in particular that are highly contagious and can cause severe illness.

- *Salmonella Typhi*
- Nontyphoidal *Salmonella* (NTS)
- *Shigella* spp.
- Shiga toxin-producing *E. coli* (STEC)

Food handlers diagnosed with illnesses from these bacteria can NEVER work in a foodservice operation while they are sick.

Bacteria: *Salmonella* Typhi (SAL-me-NEL-uh TI-fee)

Source	Food Linked with the Bacteria	Prevention Measures
Salmonella Typhi lives only in humans. People with typhoid fever carry the bacteria in their bloodstream and intestinal tract. Eating only a small amount of these bacteria can make a person sick. The severity of symptoms depends on the health of the person and the amount of bacteria eaten. The bacteria are often in a person's feces for weeks after symptoms have ended.	• Ready-to-eat food • Beverages	• Exclude food handlers who have been diagnosed with an illness caused by *Salmonella* Typhi from the operation. • Wash hands. • Cook food to minimum internal temperatures.

Bacteria: Nontyphoidal *Salmonella* (SAL-me-NEL-uh)

Source	Food Linked with the Bacteria	Prevention Measures
Many farm animals carry nontyphoidal *Salmonella* naturally. Eating only a small amount of these bacteria can make a person sick. How severe symptoms are depends on the health of the person and the amount of bacteria eaten. The bacteria are often in a person's feces for weeks after symptoms have ended.	• Poultry and eggs • Meat • Milk and dairy products • Produce, such as tomatoes, peppers, and cantaloupes	• Cook poultry and eggs to minimum internal temperatures. • Prevent cross-contamination between poultry and ready-to-eat food. • Keep food handlers who are vomiting or have diarrhea and have been diagnosed with an illness from nontyphoidal *Salmonella* out of the operation.

Bacteria: *Shigella* spp. (shi-GEL-uh)

Source	Food Linked with the Bacteria	Prevention Measures
Shigella spp. is found in the feces of humans with the illness. Most illnesses occur when people eat or drink contaminated food or water. Flies can also transfer the bacteria from feces to food. Eating only a small amount of these bacteria can make a person sick. High levels of the bacteria are often in a person's feces for weeks after symptoms have ended.	• Food that is easily contaminated by hands, such as salads containing TCS food (potato, tuna, shrimp, macaroni, and chicken) • Food that has made contact with contaminated water, such as produce	• Exclude food handlers who have diarrhea and have been diagnosed with an illness caused by *Shigella* spp. from the operation. • Wash hands. • Control flies inside and outside the operation.

Bacteria: Shiga toxin-producing *Escherichia coli* (ess-chur-EE-kee-UH-KO-LI) (STEC), also known as *E.coli*		
Source	Food Linked with the Bacteria	Prevention Measures
Shiga toxin-producing *E. coli* can be found in the intestines of cattle. It is also found in infected people. The bacteria can contaminate meat during slaughtering. Eating only a small amount of the bacteria can make a person sick. Once eaten, it produces toxins in the intestines, which cause the illness. The bacteria are often in a person's feces for weeks after symptoms have ended.	• Ground beef (raw and undercooked) • Contaminated produce	• Exclude food handlers who have diarrhea and have been diagnosed with a disease from the bacteria. • Cook food, especially ground beef, to minimum internal temperatures. • Purchase produce from approved, reputable suppliers. • Prevent cross-contamination between raw meat and ready-to-eat food.

Viruses

Viruses share some basic characteristics.

Location   Viruses are carried by human beings and animals. They require a living host to grow. While viruses do not grow in food, they can be transferred through food and still remain infectious in food.

Sources   People can get viruses from food, water, or any contaminated surface. Foodborne illnesses from viruses typically occur through fecal-oral routes. Norovirus is one of the leading causes of foodborne illness. It is often transmitted through airborne vomit particles.

Destruction   Viruses are not destroyed by normal cooking temperatures. That's why it is important to practice good personal hygiene when handling food and food-contact surfaces. The quick removal and cleanup of vomit is also important.

Major Viruses that Cause Foodborne Illness

The FDA has identified two viruses in particular that are highly contagious and can cause severe illness.

• Hepatitis A

• Norovirus

Food handlers diagnosed with hepatitis A or Norovirus must not work in a foodservice operation while they are sick.

Virus: Hepatitis A		
Source	Food Linked with the Virus	Prevention Measures
Hepatitis A is mainly found in the feces of people infected with it. The virus can contaminate water and many types of food. It is commonly linked with ready-to-eat food. However, it has also been linked with shellfish from contaminated water. The virus is often transferred to food when infected food handlers touch food or equipment with fingers that have feces on them. Eating only a small amount of the virus can make a person sick. An infected person may not show symptoms for weeks but can be very infectious. Cooking does not destroy hepatitis A.	• Ready-to-eat food • Shellfish from contaminated water	• Exclude staff who have been diagnosed with hepatitis A from the operation. • Exclude staff who have jaundice from the operation. • Wash hands. • Avoid bare-hand contact with ready-to-eat food. • Purchase shellfish from approved, reputable suppliers.

Virus: Norovirus		
Source	Food Linked with the Virus	Prevention Measures
Like hepatitis A, Norovirus is commonly linked with ready-to-eat food. It has also been linked with contaminated water. Norovirus is often transferred to food when infected food handlers touch food or equipment with fingers that have feces on them. Eating only a small amount of Norovirus can make a person sick. It is also very contagious. People become contagious within a few hours after eating it. The virus is often in a person's feces for days after symptoms have ended.	• Ready-to-eat food • Shellfish from contaminated water	• Exclude staff who are vomiting or have diarrhea and have been diagnosed with Norovirus from the operation. • Wash hands. • Avoid bare-hand contact with ready-to-eat food. • Purchase shellfish from approved, reputable suppliers.

Parasites

Parasites share some basic characteristics.

Location   Parasites require a host to live and reproduce.

Sources   Parasites are commonly associated with seafood, wild game, and food processed with contaminated water, such as produce.

Prevention   The most important way to prevent foodborne illnesses from parasites is to purchase food from approved, reputable suppliers. Cooking food to required minimum internal temperatures is also important. Make sure that fish that will be served raw or undercooked has been correctly frozen by the manufacturer.

Fungi

Fungi include yeasts, molds, and mushrooms. Some molds and mushrooms produce toxins that cause foodborne illness. Throw out all moldy food, unless the mold is a natural part of the food. Because harmful mushrooms are difficult to recognize, you must purchase all mushrooms from approved, reputable suppliers.

Biological Toxins

Most foodborne illnesses are caused by pathogens, a form of biological contamination. But you also must be aware of biological toxins or poisons that can make people sick.

Origin   Some toxins are naturally associated with certain plants, mushrooms, and seafood. Toxins are a natural part of some fish. Other toxins, such as histamine, are made by pathogens on the fish when it is time-temperature abused. This can occur in tuna, bonito, mackerel, and mahimahi. Some fish become contaminated when they eat smaller fish that have eaten a toxin. One of these toxins is the ciguatera toxin. It can be found in barracuda, snapper, grouper, and amberjack. Shellfish, such as oysters, can be contaminated when they eat marine algae that have a toxin.

Symptoms   Many types of illnesses can occur from eating seafood toxins. Each of these has specific symptoms and onset times. In general, however, people will experience an illness within minutes of eating the toxin. Depending upon the illness, symptoms can include diarrhea or vomiting. Neurological symptoms may also appear, such as tingling in the extremities and the reversal of hot and cold sensations. People may also experience flushing of the face, difficulty breathing, burning in the mouth, heart palpitations, and hives.

Prevention   Toxins cannot be destroyed by cooking or freezing. The most important way to prevent a foodborne illness is to purchase plants, mushrooms, and seafood from approved, reputable suppliers. It is also important to control time and temperature when handling raw fish.

Other Pathogens

The pathogens discussed throughout this chapter are not the only ones that can cause a foodborne illness. See the appendix for a comprehensive list of pathogens that can affect food safety.

Chemical Contaminants

Many people have gotten sick after consuming food and beverages contaminated with foodservice chemicals. To keep food safe, follow these guidelines.

Sources   Chemicals can contaminate food if they are used or stored the wrong way. Cleaners, sanitizers, polishes, machine lubricants, and pesticides can be risks. Also included are deodorizers, first-aid products, and health and beauty products, such as hand lotions and hairsprays. Certain types of kitchenware and equipment can be risks for chemical contamination. These include items made from pewter, copper, zinc, and some types of painted pottery. An example is shown at left. These materials are not food grade and can contaminate food. This is especially true when acidic food, such as tomato sauce, is held in them.

Symptoms   Symptoms vary depending on the chemical consumed. Most illnesses occur within minutes. Vomiting and diarrhea are typical. If an illness is suspected, call the emergency number in your area and the Poison Control number. Consult the chemical's Material Safety Data Sheet (MSDS), which contains important safety information about the chemical.

Prevention   The chemicals you use must be approved for use in a foodservice operation. They must also be necessary for the maintenance of the facility. Here are some ways to protect food and food-contact surfaces from contamination by chemicals.

* Purchase chemicals from approved, reputable suppliers.

* Store chemicals away from prep areas, food-storage areas, and service areas. Chemicals must be separated from food and food-contact surfaces by spacing and partitioning. Chemicals must NEVER be stored above food or food-contact surfaces.

* Use chemicals for their intended use and follow manufacturer's directions.

* Only handle food with equipment and utensils approved for foodservice use.

* Make sure the manufacturer's labels on original chemical containers are readable, as shown in the photo at left.

* Keep MSDS current, and make sure they are accessible to staff at all times.

* Follow the manufacturer's directions and local regulatory requirements when throwing out chemicals.

Physical Contaminants

Food can become contaminated when objects get into it. It can also happen when natural objects are left in food, like bones in a fish fillet.

Sources   Some common objects that can get into food include metal shavings from cans, wood, fingernails, staples, bandages, glass, jewelry, and dirt. Naturally occurring objects, such as fruit pits and bones, can also be contaminants.

Symptoms   Mild to fatal injuries are possible. This could include cuts, dental damage, and choking. Bleeding and pain may be the most outward symptoms.

Prevention   Purchase food from approved, reputable suppliers to prevent physical contamination. Closely inspect the food you receive. Take steps to make sure no physical contaminants can get into it. This includes making sure that food handlers practice good personal hygiene.

Apply Your Knowledge

Which Ones Are Contaminants?

Write an ✗ next to each item that can be a physical contaminant.

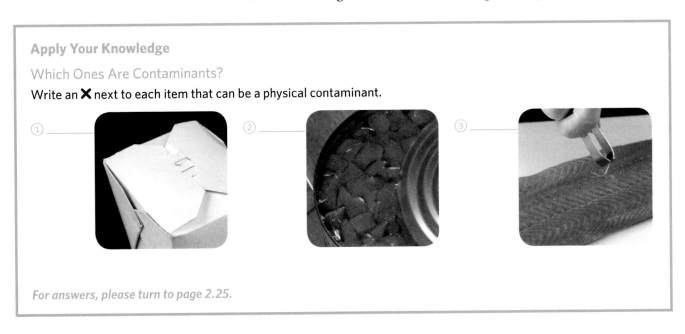

① _____   ② _____   ③ _____

For answers, please turn to page 2.25.

Apply Your Knowledge

What's Wrong with This Picture?

Write an ✘ next to each picture that shows an unsafe practice when handling chemicals.

① _____    ② _____    ③ _____

What Have I Got?

Write an ✘ next to the most common symptoms of foodborne illness.

① _____ Headache   ⑤ _____ Vomiting

② _____ Diarrhea   ⑥ _____ Nausea

③ _____ Muscle pain   ⑦ _____ Jaundice

④ _____ Fever   ⑧ _____ Sweating

What's It Stand For?

Each letter below stands for a condition that supports the growth of pathogens.
Complete the word for each letter in the space provided.

① F_____   ④ T_____

② A_____   ⑤ O_____

③ T_____   ⑥ M_____

For answers, please turn to page 2.25.

Apply Your Knowledge

Who Am I?

Identify the pathogen from the description given and write its name in the space provided.

① _____

- I am commonly linked with ready-to-eat food.
- I am found in the feces of infected people.
- Excluding staff with jaundice can stop me.
- Handwashing can prevent me.

② _____

- I am carried in the bloodstream and intestinal tract of humans.
- I am commonly linked with beverages and ready-to-eat food.
- Cooking food correctly can prevent me.
- Washing hands can stop me.

③ _____

- I am found in the intestines of cattle.
- I produce toxins in a person's intestines.
- Purchasing produce from approved suppliers can prevent me.
- Cooking ground beef correctly can stop me.

④ _____

- Flies can spread me.
- I am linked to salads containing TCS food.
- I am found in the feces of infected people.
- Washing hands can stop me.

⑤ _____

- Many farm animals carry me naturally.
- I have been found in milk and dairy products, produce, and poultry.
- Cooking eggs to minimum internal temperatures can prevent me.
- Preventing cross-contamination between poultry and ready-to-eat food can stop me.

What's the Best Way to Control Them?

Write the letter of the most important prevention measure for each pathogen in the space provided. Some letters may be used more than once.

① _____ Bacteria

② _____ Viruses

③ _____ Parasites

④ _____ Fungi

⑤ _____ Plant toxins

⑥ _____ Mushroom toxins

⑦ _____ Seafood toxins

Ⓐ Control time and temperature

Ⓑ Practice correct personal hygiene

Ⓒ Purchase from approved, reputable suppliers

For answers, please turn to page 2.25.

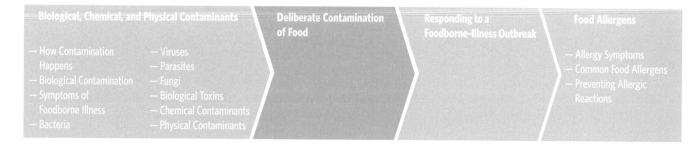

Biological, Chemical, and Physical Contaminants

— How Contamination Happens
— Biological Contamination
— Symptoms of Foodborne Illness
— Bacteria
— Viruses
— Parasites
— Fungi
— Biological Toxins
— Chemical Contaminants
— Physical Contaminants

Deliberate Contamination of Food

Responding to a Foodborne-Illness Outbreak

Food Allergens

— Allergy Symptoms
— Common Food Allergens
— Preventing Allergic Reactions

Deliberate Contamination of Food

So far, you have learned about methods to prevent the accidental contamination of food. But you also must take steps to stop people who are actually trying to contaminate it. This may include the following groups.

- Terrorists or activists
- Disgruntled current or former staff
- Vendors
- Competitors

These people may try to tamper with your food using biological, chemical, or physical contaminants. They may even use radioactive materials. Attacks might occur anywhere in the food supply chain. But they are usually focused on a specific food item, process, or business.

The best way to protect food is to make it as difficult as possible for someone to tamper with it. For this reason, a food defense program should deal with the points in your operation where food is at risk. The FDA has created a tool that can be used to develop a food defense program. It is based on the acronym A.L.E.R.T. It can be used to help you identify the points in your operation where food is at risk.

Assure   Make sure that products you receive are from safe sources.

- Supervise product deliveries.
- Use approved suppliers who practice food defense.
- Request that delivery vehicles are locked or sealed.

Look   Monitor the security of products in the facility.

- Limit access to prep and storage areas. Locking storage areas is one way to do this, as shown in the photo at left.
- Create a system for handling damaged products.
- Store chemicals in a secure location.
- Train staff to spot food defense threats.

Employees   Know who is in your facility.

- Limit access to prep and storage areas.
- Identify all visitors, and verify credentials.
- Conduct background checks on staff.

Reports   Keep information related to food defense accessible.

- Receiving logs

- Office files and documents

- Staff files

- Random food defense self-inspections

Threat   Identify what you will do and who you will contact if there is suspicious activity or a threat at your operation.

- Hold any product you suspect to be contaminated.

- Contact your regulatory authority immediately.

- Maintain an emergency contact list.

Something to Think About...

The 1984 Rajneeshee Bioterror Attack

In the fall of 1984, the single largest bioterrorist attack in the United States occurred in Oregon. It was carried out by members of a cult who had hoped to influence the turnout of a local election. They sprinkled *Salmonella* Typhimurium on salad bars at 10 local restaurants. As a result, over 750 people got sick, with 45 being hospitalized. The victims suffered from symptoms including fever, chills, diarrhea, nausea, and vomiting. Most had abdominal pain, diarrhea, and bloody stools. Fortunately, there were no fatalities.

Those responsible for the attacks spread a liquid containing the pathogen over the food on the salad bars. They also poured the liquid into the salad dressing.

Apply Your Knowledge

The Best Defense

Write an ✗ next to the practices that may be a risk to food defense.

①_____ Allowing delivery drivers to store products in coolers

②_____ Purchasing produce from local farmers markets

③_____ Giving tours of the kitchen to the general public

④_____ Giving staff access to all storage areas

⑤_____ Installing a screen door at the back of the establishment to allow cool air inside

⑥_____ Allowing vendors to deliver food from trucks that have been unlocked

⑦_____ Locking storage areas

⑧_____ Holding products you suspect are contaminated

⑨_____ Storing chemicals in a locked storage area

⑩_____ Limiting access to prep areas

For answers, please turn to page 2.25.

Biological, Chemical, and Physical Contaminants		Deliberate Contamination of Food	Responding to a Foodborne-Illness Outbreak	Food Allergens
— How Contamination Happens — Biological Contamination — Symptoms of Foodborne Illness — Bacteria	— Viruses — Parasites — Fungi — Biological Toxins — Chemical Contaminants — Physical Contaminants			— Allergy Symptoms — Common Food Allergens — Preventing Allergic Reactions

Responding to a Foodborne-Illness Outbreak

Despite your best efforts, a foodborne-illness outbreak may occur. Here are some things you should consider when responding to an outbreak.

Gathering information   Ask the person making the complaint for general contact information and to identify the food that was eaten. Also ask for a description of symptoms and when the person first became sick.

Notifying authorities   Contact the local regulatory authority if you suspect an outbreak.

Segregating product   Set the suspected product aside if any remains. Include a label with Do Not Use and Do Not Discard on it, as shown in the photo at left.

Documenting information   Log information about the suspected product. This might include a product description, production date, and lot number. The sell-by date and pack size should also be recorded.

Identifying staff   Maintain a list of food handlers scheduled at the time of the suspected contamination. These staff members may be subject to an interview and sampling by investigators. They should also be interviewed immediately by management about their health status.

Cooperating with authorities   Cooperate with regulatory authorities in the investigation. Provide appropriate documentation. You may be asked to provide temperature logs, HACCP documents, staff files, etc.

Reviewing procedures   Review food handling procedures to identify if standards are not being met or procedures are not working.

Apply Your Knowledge

What Did Phillip Do Wrong?

Read the story below and determine what Phillip did wrong.

Philip was the kitchen manager at Stacy's on 44, a diner just off of Route 44 in upstate Wisconsin. His boss, the owner/operator, had taken the day off to visit her family. So, on Monday afternoon, Philip was the manager on duty.

Just after the lunch shift slowed down, the calls began to come in. Customers were complaining that they had gotten sick after eating at the diner on Saturday. The cashier turned over the phone calls to Philip. He became a little panicked after the third call came in.

Callers told Phillip that they were experiencing diarrhea and fever. Many complained about severe vomiting as well. All of the callers had eaten the meat loaf platter. Phillip didn't know what to say. He asked them to call back the next day when the owner could help. Phillip tried to reach the owner, but his calls went straight to voice mail.

Phillip tried to remember who was working on Saturday. He thought about the ingredients in the meat loaf and what might have happened. Just as he was about to write some information down, a health inspector arrived. The inspector told Phillip that they had received illness complaints from customers who had eaten at the diner. The inspector asked Philip what information he had received from the customers who had gotten sick. He also advised Phillip that they should work together to identify the source and take action immediately. Philip said he didn't know what had happened and that he was just the kitchen manager covering the shift for his boss. He told the inspector to come back on Tuesday when the owner would be back.

What did Philip do wrong?

_____

_____

_____

_____

_____

_____

_____

_____

_____

For answers, please turn to page 2.26.

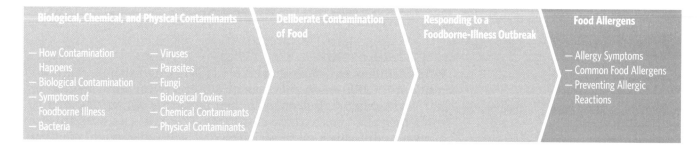

Biological, Chemical, and Physical Contaminants

— How Contamination Happens
— Biological Contamination
— Symptoms of Foodborne Illness
— Bacteria
— Viruses
— Parasites
— Fungi
— Biological Toxins
— Chemical Contaminants
— Physical Contaminants

Deliberate Contamination of Food

Responding to a Foodborne-Illness Outbreak

Food Allergens

— Allergy Symptoms
— Common Food Allergens
— Preventing Allergic Reactions

Food Allergens

A food allergen is a protein in a food or ingredient that some people are sensitive to. These proteins occur naturally. When enough of an allergen is eaten, the immune system mistakenly considers it harmful and attacks the food protein. This can result in an allergic reaction. There are specific signs that a customer is having an allergic reaction. To protect your customers, you should be able to recognize these signs and know what to do. You also should know the types of food that most often cause allergic reactions to help prevent them from happening.

Allergy Symptoms

Depending on the person, an allergic reaction can happen just after the food is eaten or several hours later. This reaction could include some or all of these symptoms.

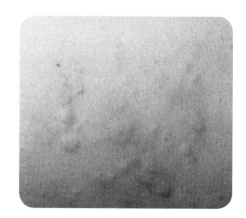

- Nausea
- Wheezing or shortness of breath
- Hives or itchy rashes, as shown in the photo at left
- Swelling of various parts of the body, including the face, eyes, hands, or feet
- Vomiting and/or diarrhea
- Abdominal pain

Initially symptoms may be mild, but they can become serious quickly. In severe cases, anaphylaxis—a severe allergic reaction that can lead to death—may result. If a customer is having a severe allergic reaction to food, call the emergency number in your area and inform them of the allergic reaction.

Common Food Allergens

You and your staff must be aware of the most common food allergens and the menu items that contain them.

While more than 160 food items can cause allergic reactions, just eight of those account for 90 percent of all reactions in the United States. These eight food items are known as the Big Eight.

- Milk
- Eggs
- Fish, such as bass, flounder, and cod
- Wheat
- Soy
- Peanuts
- Crustacean shellfish, such as crab, lobster, and shrimp
- Tree nuts, such as walnuts, and pecans

Preventing Allergic Reactions

Fifteen million Americans have a food allergy, and allergic reactions result in 200,000 emergency room visits every year. Both service staff and kitchen staff need to do their parts to avoid serving food containing allergens to these customers. These policies would also apply to addressing food sensitivities that a customer might mention, such as a gluten intolerance.

Food Labels

Calories per gram:
Fat 9 • Carbohydrate 4 • Protein 4

INGREDIENTS: CHICKEN BROTH, CONTAINS LE
OF THE FOLLOWING: SALT, DEXTROSE, CH
MONOSODIUM GLUTAMATE, HYDROLYZED WHI
NATURAL FLAVORS, AUTOLYZED YEAST EXTRA
JUICE CONCENTRATE, MONO AND DIGLYCERIDE
GUM, ONION JUICE CONCENTRATE.

CONTAINS: WHEAT.

Food labels on the products that you purchase are an important tool to identify allergens in the operation. Federal law requires manufactured products containing one or more of the Big Eight allergens to clearly identify them on the ingredient label. The allergen may be included in the common name of the food, such as "buttermilk", or it may be shown in parentheses after the ingredient. Often, allergens will be shown in a contains statement, such as in the photo to the left.

Service Staff

Your staff should be able to tell customers about menu items that contain potential allergens. At minimum, have one person available per shift to answer customers' questions about menu items. When customers say they have a food allergy, your staff should take it seriously. When working with a customer to place an allergen special order, they must be able to do the following.

Describing dishes   Tell customers how the item is prepared. Sauces, marinades, and garnishes often contain allergens. For example, peanut butter is sometimes used as a thickener in sauces or marinades. This information is critical to a customer with a peanut allergy.

Identifying ingredients   Tell customers if the food they are allergic to is in the menu item. Identify any "secret" ingredients. For example, your operation may have a house specialty that includes an allergen.

Suggesting items   Suggest menu items that do not contain the food that the customer is allergic to.

Identify the allergen special order   Clearly mark or otherwise indicate the order for the guest with the identified food allergy. This is done to inform the kitchen staff of the guest's food allergy.

Delivering food   Confirm the allergen special order with the kitchen staff when picking up the food. Make sure no garnishes or other items containing the allergen touch the plate. Food should be hand-delivered to guests with allergies. Delivering food separately from the other food delivered to a table, as shown in the photo at left, will help prevent contact with food allergens.

Kitchen Staff

Staff must make sure that allergens are not transferred from food containing an allergen to the food served to the customer. This is called cross-contact. Here are a few examples of how it can happen.

- Cooking different types of food in the same fryer oil can cause cross-contact. In the photo at left, shrimp allergens could be transferred to the chicken being fried in the same oil.
- Letting food touch surfaces, equipment, or utensils that have touched allergens can cause cross-contact. For example, putting chocolate chip cookies on the same parchment paper that was used for peanut butter cookies can transfer some of the peanut allergen.

How to Avoid Cross-Contact

- Check recipes and ingredient labels to confirm that the allergen is not present.
- Wash, rinse, and sanitize cookware, utensils, and equipment before prepping food, as shown in the photo at left. This includes food-prep surfaces. Some operations use a separate set of cooking utensils just for allergen special orders.
- Make sure the allergen does not touch anything for customers with food allergies, including food, beverages, utensils, equipment, and gloves.
- Wash your hands and change gloves before prepping food.
- Use separate fryers and cooking oils when frying food for customers with food allergies.
- Label food packaged on-site for retail sale. Name all major allergens on the label and follow any additional labeling requirements.

Apply Your Knowledge

Identify the Symptoms

Write an ✖ next to the symptoms that could indicate a customer is having an allergic reaction.

1. _____ Nausea
2. _____ Bruising
3. _____ Sneezing
4. _____ Coughing
5. _____ Itchy rash

6. _____ Hives
7. _____ Swollen face
8. _____ Abdominal pain
9. _____ Swollen abdomen
10. _____ Increased appetite

11. _____ Shortness of breath
12. _____ Tightening in the chest
13. _____ Tingling in arms
14. _____ Diarrhea

The Most Common Food Allergens

Write an ✖ next to a food if it is or has a common food allergen.

1. _____ Tea
2. _____ Cod
3. _____ Wheat flour
4. _____ Melons
5. _____ Peanut butter
6. _____ Crab legs

7. _____ Potatoes
8. _____ Mushrooms
9. _____ Tomatoes
10. _____ Pecan pie
11. _____ Citrus fruit
12. _____ Green peppers

13. _____ Squash and eggplant
14. _____ Soybeans
15. _____ Rice and rice products
16. _____ Omelet
17. _____ Vanilla ice cream

For answers, please turn to page 2.26.

Chapter Summary

- Contamination is the presence of harmful substances in food. Those substances can be biological, chemical, or physical.

- Pathogens are disease-causing microorganisms that make you sick when you eat them. Others produce poisons—or toxins—that make you sick. There are four types of pathogens that can contaminate food and cause foodborne illness. These are viruses, bacteria, parasites, and fungi.

- Some common symptoms of foodborne illness include diarrhea, vomiting, fever, nausea, abdominal cramps, and jaundice. Onset times will depend on the type of foodborne illness a person has.

- Bacteria cannot be seen, smelled, or tasted. If conditions are correct, bacteria will grow rapidly. The most important prevention measure is to control time and temperature. Bacteria need six conditions to grow. They can be remembered by the word FAT TOM. It stands for food, acidity, temperature, time, oxygen, and moisture. You will most likely be able to control only time and temperature.

- *Salmonella* Typhi, nontyphoidal *Salmonella*, *Shigella* spp., and shiga toxin-producing *E. coli* (STEC) are highly contagious and can cause severe illness.

- Viruses require a host to grow. People can get viruses from food, water, or contaminated surfaces. Many viruses are transferred through the fecal-oral route. Most are not destroyed by normal cooking temperatures. That's why it's important to practice good personal hygiene when handling food and food-contact surfaces.

- Hepatitis A and Norovirus are highly contagious and can cause severe illness.

- Parasites require a host to live and reproduce. They are commonly associated with seafood and food processed with contaminated water. The most important measure for preventing parasites from causing a foodborne illness is to purchase food from approved, reputable suppliers. Fungi include mold, yeasts, and mushrooms. Like parasites, they are prevented by purchasing food from approved, reputable suppliers.

- Some toxins cannot be destroyed by cooking or freezing. The most important way to prevent a foodborne illness is to purchase plants, mushrooms, and seafood from approved, reputable suppliers. It is also important to control time and temperature when handling raw fish.

- Chemical contaminants include toxic metals, cleaners, sanitizers, polishes, and machine lubricants. To help prevent chemical contamination, store chemicals away from prep areas, food storage areas, and service areas. Always follow the manufacturers' directions when using chemicals.

- Physical contamination can happen when objects get into food. Naturally occurring objects, such as bones in a fish fillet, are a physical hazard. Closely inspect the food you receive. Make sure no physical contaminants can get into it at any point during the flow of food.

- People may try to tamper with food using biological, chemical, physical, or even radioactive contaminants. The key to protecting food is to make it hard for someone to tamper with it.

- A food allergen is a naturally occurring protein in a food or ingredient that some people are sensitive to. The most common food allergens include milk, eggs, soy, fish, tree nuts, peanuts, crustacean shellfish, and wheat. Service staff must be able to tell customers about menu items that contain potential allergens. Kitchen staff must make sure that allergens are not transferred from food containing an allergen to the food served to the customer with allergies.

Chapter Review Case Study

Now, take what you have learned in this chapter and apply it to the following case study.

An e-mail alert had just come from company headquarters. It seemed that a foodborne-illness outbreak had occurred at two company operations in the southern district.

Byron was the general manager of the highest volume operation in the chain's northern district. When he got the e-mail alert, he became very concerned. All of the food, recipes, and food handling procedures were the same company-wide. All of the food products came from the company's central commissary. Recipes came down from the corporate chef. And, food safety policies and procedures were taught by the same instructors. Byron was worried. He wondered if something could happen in his operation. Because everything was done the same way company-wide, he was very concerned about a potential outbreak.

Byron decided to gather his team of managers and discuss what was going on. He filled them in on the details of the outbreak at the other stores. He then asked the team what they thought could be done to prevent it from occurring in their operation.

Byron's executive chef, Amelia, said that she would double-check if all of the food safety procedures were being followed by her staff. She also suggested taking a closer look at how they could set up barriers to foodborne illness. She suggested that they review FAT TOM.

Byron and the other managers looked at each other and wondered what she was talking about. Chef Amelia explained that the words FAT TOM were a good way of remembering the conditions bacteria need to grow. She said that if FAT TOM could be controlled, then foodborne illness could be prevented. She went on to explain what each letter of FAT TOM meant. The team began to work on a complete review of all the aspects of FAT TOM with Byron's and Amelia's supervision. They focused specifically on time and temperature control.

① What did Byron do correctly?

_____

_____

② Why was Chef Amelia's review of FAT TOM important in helping keep food safe in the operation?

_____

_____

_____

For answers, please turn to page 2.26.

Study Questions

Circle the best answer to each question.

1. **What are the most common symptoms of a foodborne illness?**

   A Diarrhea, vomiting, fever, nausea, abdominal cramps, and dizziness

   B Diarrhea, vomiting, fever, nausea, abdominal cramps, and headache

   C Diarrhea, vomiting, fever, nausea, abdominal cramps, and jaundice

   D Diarrhea, vomiting, fever, nausea, abdominal cramps, and tiredness

2. **What is the most important way to prevent a foodborne illness from bacteria?**

   A Control time and temperature.

   B Prevent cross-contamination.

   C Practice good personal hygiene.

   D Practice good cleaning and sanitizing.

3. **Shiga toxin-producing *E. coli* (STEC) is commonly linked with what type of food?**

   A Potato salad

   B Thick stews

   C Dairy products

   D Raw ground beef

4. **What is the most important way to prevent a foodborne illness from viruses?**

   A Control time and temperature.

   B Prevent cross-contamination.

   C Practice good personal hygiene.

   D Practice good cleaning and sanitizing.

5. **A guest called a restaurant and told the manager about getting sick after eating there. The guest complained of vomiting and diarrhea a few hours after eating the raw oysters. What pathogen probably caused the illness?**

   A Norovirus

   B *Shigella* spp.

   C *Salmonella* Typhi

   D Shiga toxin-producing *E. coli*

Continued on the next page ▶

► *Continued from previous page*

⑥ **Parasites are commonly linked with what type of food?**

A Rice

B Poultry

C Seafood

D Canned food

⑦ **A guest had a reversal of hot and cold sensations after eating seafood. What most likely caused the illness?**

A Toxin

B Virus

C Bacteria

D Parasite

⑧ **A food handler stored a sanitizer spray bottle on the shelf above the prep table that had just been sanitized. Throughout the day, the food handler used the sanitizer on the prep table, storing it in the same spot. What should the food handler have done differently?**

A Stored the sanitizer bottle away from the prep area

B Stored the sanitizer bottle on the floor between uses

C Stored the sanitizer bottle on the prep table between uses

D Stored the sanitizer bottle with food supplies below the prep table

⑨ **To prevent the deliberate contamination of food, a manager should know who is in the facility, monitor the security of products, keep information related to food security on file, and know**

A when to register with the EPA.

B how to fill out an incident report.

C where to find MSDS in the operation.

D who to contact about suspicious activity.

⑩ **What should food handlers do to prevent food allergens from being transferred to food?**

A Clean and sanitize utensils after use.

B Buy from approved, reputable suppliers.

C Store cold food at 41°F (5°C) or lower.

D Label chemical containers correctly.

For answers, please turn to page 2.26.

Answers

2.10 Which Ones Are Contaminants?

1, 2, and 3 should be marked. The container of Chinese food in photo 1 has been stapled shut. The staple can easily end up in the food. The can opener has left metal shavings in the canned food in photo 2. The food handler is pulling out bones from a fish filet in photo 3. All of these are physical contaminants.

2.11 What's Wrong with This Picture?

1, 2, and 3 should be marked. The food handler in photo 1 is using the glass cleaner incorrectly by spraying it near food. The chemical spray bottle in photo 2 does not contain a label with the common name of the chemical. The chemicals in photo 3 are being stored above food.

2.11 What Have I Got?

2, 4, 5, 6, and 7 should be marked.

2.11 What's It Stand For?

① Food

② Acidity

③ Temperature

④ Time

⑤ Oxygen

⑥ Moisture

2.12 Who Am I?

① Hepatitis A

② *Salmonella* Typhi

③ Shiga toxin-producing *E. coli* (STEC)

④ *Shigella* spp.

⑤ Nontyphoidal *Salmonella*

2.12 What's the Best Way to Control Them?

① A   ⑤ C

② B   ⑥ C

③ C   ⑦ C

④ C

2.14 The Best Defense

1 through 6 should be marked.

Continued on the next page ▶

▶ *Continued from previous page*

2.16   What Did Philip Do Wrong?

- He failed to gather general contact information from the customers who called.
- He failed to notify the local regulatory authority of the suspected outbreak.
- He failed to segregate any suspected product.
- He failed to document information about the suspected product.
- He failed to identify staff who may have been in contact with the suspected product.
- He failed to cooperate with authorities.

2.19   Identify the Symptoms

1, 5, 6, 7, 8, 11, and 14 should be marked.

2.19   The Most Common Food Allergens

2, 3, 5, 6, 10, 14, 16, and 17 should be marked.

2.22   Chapter Review Case Study

① What did Byron do correctly?

- He was concerned about reports of foodborne illness from other company operations.
- He gathered his team to review food safety procedures and see if anything extra could be done to help keep food safe.

② Why was Chef Amelia's review of FAT TOM important in helping keep food safe in the operation?

- Bacteria need six conditions to grow which are represented by the six letters in the words, FAT TOM. They stand for Food, Acidity, Time, Temperature, Oxygen, and Moisture. Chef Amelia realized that by controlling FAT TOM in her operation, she could control the growth of bacteria. This could help prevent foodborne illness.
- You can help keep food safe by controlling FAT TOM. In most operations, however, you will most likely be able to control only time and temperature. To control temperature, you must do your best to keep TCS food out of the temperature danger zone. To control time, you must limit how long food spends in the temperature danger zone.

2.23   Study Questions

① C	⑤ A	⑨ D
② A	⑥ C	⑩ A
③ D	⑦ A	
④ C	⑧ A	

Notes

chapter 3
The Safe Food Handler

How Food Handlers Can Contaminate Food		A Good Personal Hygiene Program		
— Situations That Can Lead to Contaminating Food — Actions That Can Contaminate Food	— Managing a Personal Hygiene Program — Handwashing — Hand Care	— Single-Use Gloves — Bare-Hand Contact with Ready-to-Eat Food — Personal Cleanliness — Work Attire	— Eating, Drinking, Smoking, and Chewing Gum or Tobacco	— Policies for Reporting Health Issues — Handling Staff Illnesses

((NEWS)) Hepatitis A Scare

Hepatitis A vaccinations were offered to thousands of guests who had visited a local casual-dining restaurant in the Gulf Coast region of the United States. The vaccinations were made available by the local regulatory authority after a food handler at the restaurant tested positive for hepatitis A, exposing the guests to the virus. The identified food handler was responsible for preparing and setting up items on the restaurant's salad bar.

The food handler was excluded from work until approved to return by a physician and the regulatory authority. The local regulatory authority also worked with the restaurant to ensure it had all of the correct processes in place to protect guests and the team.

You Can Prevent This

The incident in the story above could have been avoided if the illness had been reported to the manager once the food handler started experiencing symptoms. You can prevent a situation like this by requiring staff to report any health problems before they come to work. Reporting illness is just one part of a good personal hygiene program. The program should also address these areas.

- Avoiding personal behaviors that can contaminate food

- Washing and caring for hands

- Dressing for work and handling work clothes

- Limiting where staff can eat, drink, smoke, and chew gum or tobacco

- Preventing staff who may be carrying pathogens from working with or around food, or from working in the operation

How Food Handlers Can Contaminate Food	A Good Personal Hygiene Program			
— Situations That Can Lead to Contaminating Food — Actions That Can Contaminate Food	— Managing a Personal Hygiene Program — Handwashing — Hand Care	— Single-Use Gloves — Bare-Hand Contact with Ready-to-Eat Food — Personal Cleanliness — Work Attire	— Eating, Drinking, Smoking, and Chewing Gum or Tobacco	— Policies for Reporting Health Issues — Handling Staff Illnesses

How Food Handlers Can Contaminate Food

At every step in the flow of food, food handlers can contaminate food. They might not even realize it when they do it. Something as simple as touching the face while prepping a salad could make a customer sick. Even a food handler who appears to be healthy may spread foodborne pathogens. As a manager, you need to know the many ways that food handlers can contaminate food.

Situations That Can Lead to Contaminating Food

Food handlers can contaminate food in any of the following situations.

- When they have a foodborne illness.

- When they have wounds that contain a pathogen.

- When sneezing or coughing.

- When they have contact with a person who is ill.

- When they touch anything that may contaminate their hands and then they don't wash them. The buser in the photo at left may have contaminated his hands and could spread pathogens if he fails to wash them.

- When they have symptoms such as diarrhea, vomiting, or jaundice—a yellowing of the eyes or skin.

With some illnesses, a person may infect other people before showing any symptoms. For example, a person could spread hepatitis A for weeks before having any symptoms. With other illnesses, a person may infect other people for days or even months after symptoms are gone. Norovirus can be spread for days after symptoms have ended.

Some people carry pathogens and infect others without ever getting sick themselves. These people are called carriers. The bacteria *Staphylococcus aureus* is a pathogen carried in the nose of 30 to 50 percent of healthy adults. About 20 to 35 percent of healthy adults carry it on their skin. Food handlers transfer this type of bacteria to food when they touch the infected areas of their bodies and then touch food without washing their hands.

Actions That Can Contaminate Food

To avoid causing a foodborne illness, pay close attention to what you do with your hands. Some common actions to avoid are:

- **A** Scratching the scalp
- **B** Running fingers through the hair
- **C** Wiping or touching the nose
- **D** Rubbing an ear
- **E** Touching a pimple or an infected wound
- **F** Wearing a dirty uniform
- **G** Coughing or sneezing into the hand
- **H** Spitting in the operation

Apply Your Knowledge

Who Is at Risk?

Write an ✗ next to the food handler's name if there is a risk that the food handler could spread pathogens.

1. _____ Jamie, a prep cook, has a habit of rubbing his chin. Even though people tease him about this, he doesn't even notice when he touches it.

2. _____ Rita, a pizza maker, has a bad headache but no fever. She gets a lot of headaches, but she always comes to work anyway.

3. _____ Lee, a sous chef, didn't have time to do laundry. He has to wear the same chef coat he wore yesterday.

4. _____ Phillip, a grill operator, has a small cut on his cheek. It's not bleeding, but he has a bandage on it.

5. _____ Gary, a dishwasher, has allergies. Sometimes he needs to spit, so he spits in the garbage can next to the sink.

6. _____ Helen's children have had diarrhea. Her mother has been caring for them so that Helen, a line cook, could go to work.

7. _____ Victor, an ice cream server, likes outdoor activities. Last weekend, he went camping in an area where there were no indoor toilets.

8. _____ Sabrina, a pastry chef, has dandruff, which itches. She tries not to scratch her head, but sometimes she just has to do it.

For answers, please turn to page 3.20.

How Food Handlers Can Contaminate Food	A Good Personal Hygiene Program			
— Situations That Can Lead to Contaminating Food — Actions That Can Contaminate Food	— Managing a Personal Hygiene Program — Handwashing — Hand Care	— Single-Use Gloves — Bare-Hand Contact with Ready-to-Eat Food — Personal Cleanliness — Work Attire	— Eating, Drinking, Smoking, and Chewing Gum or Tobacco	— Policies for Reporting Health Issues — Handling Staff Illnesses

A Good Personal Hygiene Program

To keep food handlers from contaminating food, your operation needs a good personal hygiene program. A good personal hygiene program also helps everyone feel confident in the cleanliness of the business. As a manager, you must make sure this program succeeds. You must create and support policies that address the following areas.

Ⓐ Hand practices

- Handwashing
- Hand care
- Glove use
- Preventing bare-hand contact with ready-to-eat food

Ⓑ Personal cleanliness

Ⓒ Clothing, hair restraints, and jewelry

Food handlers must also avoid certain habits and actions, maintain good health, cover wounds, and report illnesses.

Managing a Personal Hygiene Program

Don't underestimate your role in a personal hygiene program. You have many responsibilities to help make the program work.

- Creating personal hygiene policies.
- Training food handlers on those policies and retraining them regularly.
- Modeling the correct behavior at all times. The manager in the photo at left is modeling good personal hygiene practices. He is wearing clean clothes and a hair restraint. He is also using gloves.
- Supervising food safety practices at all times.
- Revising personal hygiene policies when laws or science change.

Handwashing

Handwashing is the most important part of personal hygiene. It may seem like an obvious thing to do. Even so, many food handlers do not wash their hands the correct way or as often as they should. Every day, our hands touch surfaces covered with microorganisms that we cannot see. Even healthy people can spread pathogens. You must train your food handlers to wash their hands, and then you must monitor them.

SCAN TO DOWNLOAD

GERM SCANNER

Where to Wash Hands

Hands must be washed in a sink designated for handwashing. NEVER wash hands in sinks designated for food prep, dishwashing, or utility services.

How to Wash Hands

To wash hands or prosthetic devices correctly, follow the steps shown below. The whole process should take at least 20 seconds.

❶ Wet hands and arms.

Use running water as hot as you can comfortably stand. It should be at least 100°F (38°C).

❷ Apply soap.

Apply enough to build up a good lather.

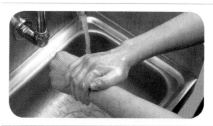

❸ Scrub hands and arms vigorously.

Scrub them for 10 to 15 seconds. Clean under fingernails and between fingers.

❹ Rinse hands and arms thoroughly.

Use running warm water.

❺ Dry hands and arms.

Use a single-use paper towel or a hand dryer.

If you are not careful, you can contaminate your hands after washing them. Consider using a paper towel to turn off the faucet and to open the door when leaving the restroom.

When to Wash Hands

Food handlers must wash their hands before they start work. They must also do it after the following activities.

- Using the restroom. Food handlers carrying pathogens, such as Norovirus, can transfer them to food if they don't wash their hands after using the restroom.

- Handling raw meat, poultry, and seafood (before and after).

- Touching the hair, face, or body.

- Sneezing, coughing, or using a tissue.

- Eating, drinking, smoking, or chewing gum or tobacco.

- Handling chemicals that might affect food safety.

- Taking out garbage.

- Clearing tables or busing dirty dishes.

- Touching clothing or aprons.

- Handling money.

- Leaving and returning to the kitchen/prep area.

- Handling service animals or aquatic animals.

- Touching anything else that may contaminate hands, such as dirty equipment, work surfaces, or cloths. The food handler in the photo at left should wash his hands after using the cloth to wipe the prep counter.

Hand Antiseptics

Hand antiseptics are liquids or gels that are used to lower the number of pathogens on skin. If used, they must comply with the Code of Federal Regulations (CFR) and Food and Drug Administration (FDA) standards.

Only use hand antiseptics after handwashing. **NEVER** use them in place of it. Wait for a hand antiseptic to dry before you touch food or equipment.

Check your local regulatory requirements.

How This Relates to Me

Are hand antiseptics allowed by your local regulatory authority?

_____ Yes   _____ No

If allowed, what are the regulatory requirements?

_____

_____

_____

Hand Care

In addition to washing, hands need other care to prevent spreading pathogens. Make sure food handlers follow these guidelines.

Fingernail length Keep fingernails short and clean. Long fingernails may be hard to keep clean and can rip gloves. They can also chip and become physical contaminants.

Fingernails should be kept trimmed and filed. This will allow nails to be cleaned easily. Ragged nails can be hard to keep clean. They may also hold pathogens and break off—becoming physical contaminants.

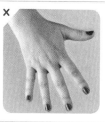

False fingernails Do **NOT** wear false fingernails. They can be hard to keep clean. False fingernails also can break off into food. Some local regulatory authorities allow false nails if single-use gloves are worn.

Nail polish Do **NOT** wear nail polish. It can disguise dirt under nails and may flake off into food. Some regulatory authorities allow polished nails if single-use gloves are worn.

Infected wounds or cuts Infected wounds, cuts, or boils contain pus. They must be covered to prevent pathogens from contaminating food and food-contact surfaces. How a wound is covered depends on where it is located.

- Cover wounds on the hand or wrist with an impermeable cover. "Impermeable" means that liquid cannot pass through the cover. Examples include bandages and finger cots. Next, place a single-use glove over the cover.
- Cover wounds on the arm with an impermeable cover, such as a bandage. The wound must be completely covered.
- Cover wounds on other parts of the body with a dry, durable, tight-fitting bandage.

Check your local regulatory requirements.

Something to Think About...

More Than They Bargained For

At an operation on the East Coast, the salad bar was very popular. One afternoon while prepping the lettuce, a food handler cut her finger. She bandaged it right away and returned to work. While she was tossing the salad, the bandage fell off into the lettuce.

A short time later, a customer reported that she had found a used bandage in her salad. The manager apologized and quickly comped her meal. Fortunately, the customer was easygoing, and the rest of the evening was uneventful.

Single-Use Gloves

Single-use gloves can help keep food safe by creating a barrier between hands and food. They should be used when handling ready-to-eat food. The exceptions include when washing produce, or when handling ready-to-eat ingredients for a dish that will be cooked to the correct internal temperature.

When buying gloves for handling food, follow these guidelines.

Approved gloves　Only gloves approved for foodservice should be purchased.

Disposable gloves　Buy only single-use gloves for handling food. **NEVER** wash and reuse gloves.

Multiple sizes　Make sure you provide different glove sizes. Gloves that are too big will not stay on. Those that are too small will tear or rip easily. The photo at left shows a correct fit.

Latex alternatives　Some food handlers and customers may be sensitive to latex. Consider providing gloves made from other materials.

How to Use Gloves

If you are not careful when using gloves, the food you handle can become unsafe. Follow these guidelines.

- Wash your hands before putting on gloves when starting a new task. You do not need to rewash your hands each time you change gloves as long as you are performing the same task, and your hands have not become contaminated.

- Select the correct glove size.

- Hold gloves by the edge when putting them on. Avoid touching the glove as much as possible.

- Once you've put them on, check the gloves for rips or tears.

- **NEVER** blow into gloves.

- **NEVER** roll gloves to make them easier to put on.

When to Change Gloves

Food handlers must change gloves at all of these times.

- As soon as they become dirty or torn.

- Before beginning a different task.

- After an interruption, such as taking a phone call.

- After handling raw meat, seafood, or poultry, and before handling ready-to-eat food.

Check your local regulatory requirements.

How This Relates to Me

What are your local regulatory requirements for glove use?

_____

_____

_____

Bare-Hand Contact with Ready-To-Eat Food

Food can become contaminated when it has been handled with bare hands. This is especially true when hands have not been washed correctly or have infected cuts or wounds. For this reason, do **NOT** handle ready-to-eat food with bare hands. **NEVER** handle ready-to-eat food with bare hands if you primarily serve a high-risk population.

There are times when it may be acceptable to handle ready-to-eat food with bare hands. This is true in the following situations.

- The food will be added as an ingredient to a dish that does not contain raw meat, seafood, or poultry, but will be cooked to at least 145°F (63°C). For example, adding cheese to pizza dough.

- The food will be added as an ingredient to a dish containing raw meat, seafood, or poultry, and the dish will be cooked to the required minimum internal temperature of the raw item(s). For example, adding vegetables to a beef stew.

Some regulatory authorities allow bare-hand contact with ready-to-eat food. If your jurisdiction allows this, you must have specific policies in place about staff health. You must also train staff in handwashing and personal hygiene practices.

Check your local regulatory requirements.

How This Relates to Me

Does your local regulatory authority allow bare-hand contact with ready-to-eat food?

_____ Yes   _____ No

If allowed, what are the regulatory requirements?

_____

_____

_____

Personal Cleanliness

Pathogens can be found on hair and skin. There is a greater risk of these pathogens being transferred to food and food equipment if the food handler does not follow a personal hygiene program. Make sure food handlers shower or bathe before work.

Work Attire

Food handlers in dirty clothes may give a bad impression of your operation. More important, dirty clothing may carry pathogens that can cause foodborne illnesses. These pathogens can be transferred from the clothing to the hands and to the food being prepared. Set up a dress code, and make sure all staff follow it. The code should include the guidelines listed on the next page.

Work Attire Guidelines

Hair restraints   Wear a clean hat or other hair restraint when in a food prep area. Do **NOT** wear hair accessories that could become physical contaminants. Hair accessories should be limited to items that keep hands out of hair, and hair out of food. False eyelashes can become physical contaminants and should **NOT** be worn. Food handlers with facial hair should also wear a beard restraint.

Clean clothing   Wear clean clothing daily. If possible, change into work clothes at work. Store street clothing and personal belongings in designated areas. Dirty clothing that is stored in the operation must be kept away from food and prep areas. You can do this by placing them in nonabsorbent containers or washable laundry bags. This includes dirty aprons, chef coats, and other uniforms.

Aprons   Remove aprons when leaving prep areas. For example, aprons should be removed and stored before taking out garbage or using the restroom.

NEVER wipe your hands on your apron.

Jewelry   Remove jewelry from hands and arms before prepping food or when working around prep areas. Food handlers cannot wear any of the following.

- Rings, except for a plain band
- Bracelets, including medical bracelets
- Watches

Your company may also require you to remove other types of jewelry. This may include earrings, necklaces, and facial jewelry. These items can fall off and become a physical contaminant. Ornate jewelry can be difficult to clean and can hold pathogens. Servers may wear jewelry if allowed by company policy.

Check your local regulatory requirements.

Eating, Drinking, Smoking, and Chewing Gum or Tobacco

Small droplets of saliva can contain thousands of pathogens. In the process of eating, drinking, smoking, or chewing gum or tobacco, saliva can be transferred to hands or directly to food being handled.

Do **NOT** eat, drink, smoke, or chew gum or tobacco at these times.

- When prepping or serving food
- When working in prep areas
- When working in areas used to clean utensils and equipment

Only eat, drink, smoke, and chew gum or tobacco in designated areas.

Some regulatory authorities allow food handlers to drink from a covered container while in prep and dishwashing areas.

Check your local regulatory requirements.

Policies for Reporting Health Issues

You must tell your staff to let you know when they are sick. This includes newly hired staff who haven't started working yet. Your regulatory authority may ask for proof that you have done this, which can be provided in the following ways.

- Presenting signed statements in which staff have agreed to report illness
- Providing documentation showing staff have completed training, which includes information on the importance of reporting illness
- Posting signs or providing pocket cards that remind staff to notify managers when they are ill

Staff must report illnesses before they come to work. They should also let you know immediately if they get sick while working, as the food handler in the photo at left is doing. When food handlers are ill, you may need to restrict them from working with or around food. Sometimes, you may need to exclude them from working in the operation. Use the following chart to help you decide how to handle staff illnesses. Note that for most illnesses, however, you should work with your local regulatory authority to determine how to respond.

Handling Staff Illnesses

If	Then
The food handler has a sore throat with a fever.	Restrict the food handler from working with or around food. Exclude the food handler from the operation if you primarily serve a high-risk population. The food handler can return to the operation and/or work with or around food when he or she has a written release from a medical practitioner.
The food handler has at least one of these symptoms from an infectious condition. • Vomiting • Diarrhea • Jaundice (yellow skin or eyes)	Exclude the food handler from the operation. **Vomiting and diarrhea** Food handlers must meet one of these requirements before they can return to work. • Have had no symptoms for at least 24 hours. • Have a written release from a medical practitioner. **Jaundice** Food handlers with jaundice must be reported to the regulatory authority. Food handlers who have had jaundice for seven days or less must be excluded from the operation. Food handlers must have a written release from a medical practitioner and approval from the regulatory authority before returning to work.
The food handler is vomiting or has diarrhea and has been diagnosed with an illness caused by one of these pathogens. • Norovirus • *Shigella* spp. • Nontyphoidal *Salmonella* • Shiga toxin-producing *E. coli* (STEC) The food handler has been diagnosed with an illness caused by one of these pathogens. • Hepatitis A • *Salmonella* Typhi	Exclude the food handler from the operation. Some food handlers diagnosed with an illness may not experience symptoms, or their symptoms may have ended. Work with the medical practitioner and the local regulatory authority to determine whether these food handlers must be excluded from the operation or restricted from working with or around food. They will also determine when the employee can safely return to the operation and/or carry out their regular food handling duties.

This chart is only a guide. Work with your local regulatory authority to determine the best course of action.

How This Relates to Me

When does your regulatory authority require food handlers to be restricted from working with or around food?

_____

What other illnesses or illness symptoms would require you to exclude a food handler from your operation?

_____

_____

Apply Your Knowledge

Check Your Handwashing Savvy

Circle the letters of the correct steps for handwashing from column A. Then put them in the correct order in column B.

Column A

Ⓐ Scrub hands and arms for 3 to 5 seconds.

Ⓑ Scrub hands and arms for 10 to 15 seconds.

Ⓒ Rinse hands and arms in warm, running water.

Ⓓ Rinse hands and arms in warm, standing water.

Ⓔ Wet hands and arms with water at least 100°F (38°C).

Ⓕ Wet hands and arms with water at least 115°F (46°C).

Ⓖ Apply enough soap to build up a good lather.

Ⓗ Apply enough soap to cover the palm of your hand.

Ⓘ Dry hands and arms on a shared towel.

Ⓙ Dry hands and arms with a single-use paper towel or hand dryer.

Column B

① _____

② _____

③ _____

④ _____

⑤ _____

For answers, please turn to page 3.20.

Apply Your Knowledge

When to Wash Hands?

Paul was just promoted from buser to prep-cook-in-training at the busy family restaurant where he has worked for nine months. Since his promotion last week, he has already learned some basic tasks. Today, Paul arrived promptly at work at 8:00 a.m. and punched in. In a preshift meeting, his manager, Miguel, told him that his first task was to tray up 60 boneless chicken breasts to be cooked later in the shift. After that, Paul was to work with Linda, an experienced prep cook.

Eager to make a good impression, Paul got the raw chicken from the cooler. He put on single-use gloves and started traying up the breasts. About halfway through, Miguel stopped by with someone in a suit, whom Miguel introduced as one of the new owners. Paul took off his gloves to shake the owner's hand. Afterwards, he put on a new pair of single-use gloves and got back to the chicken.

After Paul finished the chicken, he put it in the cooler. Then he noticed a pile of dirty dishes next to the dishwasher. He decided to help out and loaded the dishes into a dish rack. When it was full, he ran the load.

Linda came by and told him to prep vegetables for the salad bar. The salad bar needed to be set up in an hour, so Paul put on single-use gloves and got started right away. As he was chopping lettuce, Paul suddenly sneezed. Fortunately, he was able to turn away from the prep table in time. He also was able to catch the sneeze with his hand. He changed gloves and went back to chopping the lettuce. Then Paul needed a tissue. Not having one handy, he had to go to the restroom to blow his nose on toilet paper. While he was there, he also used the toilet. Then he returned to the prep area, put on new gloves, and finished prepping vegetables. He placed the prepped vegetables in the cooler.

Linda asked Paul to let the salad bar attendant know the vegetables were ready. Then she asked him to work with her on the grill during the lunch hour. She started off by showing him how to make a grilled chicken sandwich. When a second order for a grilled chicken sandwich came in, Paul got to make it. A bit nervous, he dropped the tongs for the raw chicken before he could get a piece onto the grill. Linda went to get a clean pair of tongs but got delayed by a conversation with Miguel.

Paul was sure he could make the sandwich without Linda's help. While she was talking with Miguel, he picked up a raw chicken breast with his hands and put it on the grill. Then he got out a fresh bun and put it in the toaster. Before he could finish the sandwich, Linda came back, and they finished it together. As they worked together on the orders, the lunch rush flew by.

When should Paul have washed his hands?

_____

_____

_____

_____

Exclusion or Restriction?

Write an E next to the statement if the food handler must be excluded from the operation. Write an R next to the statement if the person should be restricted from working with or around food.

① _____ Bill, a line cook at a family restaurant, has a sore throat with a fever.

② _____ Joe, a prep cook, has diarrhea.

③ _____ Mary a sous chef, has diarrhea and has been diagnosed with Norovirus.

For answers, please turn to page 3.20.

Chapter Summary

- Food handlers can spread pathogens and contaminate food at every step in the flow of food. Good personal hygiene is critical in an operation.

- Hands must be washed correctly and at the correct times: before starting work; after using the restroom; after sneezing, coughing, smoking, eating, or drinking; and before and after handling raw meat, poultry, and fish.

- Fingernails should be kept short, clean, and without polish.

- Before handling food or working in prep areas, food handlers must put on clean clothing and a clean hair restraint. They must remove jewelry from hands and arms. Aprons should be removed and stored when food handlers leave prep areas.

- Food handlers should never eat, smoke, or chew gum or tobacco in food prep or service areas, or in areas designated for cleaning utensils and equipment.

- Staff must report health problems to management before working with food. Food handlers must be excluded from work if they are vomiting or have diarrhea and have been diagnosed with a foodborne illness from certain pathogens, such as nontyphoidal *Salmonella*. Food handlers also must not come to work if they have symptoms that include diarrhea, vomiting, or jaundice. Staff should not work with or around food if they have a sore throat and a fever.

- To keep food handlers from contaminating food, your operation needs a good personal hygiene program. You can minimize the risk of foodborne illnesses by establishing a program, training, and enforcing it. Most important, you must set an example yourself by practicing good personal hygiene.

Chapter Review Case Study

You can avoid spreading pathogens to food if you follow a good personal hygiene program. This includes avoiding personal behaviors that can contaminate food; washing and caring for hands; following a dress code; limiting where food handlers can eat, drink, smoke, and chew gum or tobacco; and preventing food handlers who may be carrying pathogens from working with or around food, or, if necessary, excluding them from the operation.

Now, take what you have learned in this chapter and apply it to the following case study.

Randall is a food handler at a deli. It is 7:47 a.m., and he has just woken up. He is scheduled to be at work and ready to go by 8:00 a.m. When he gets out of bed, his stomach feels queasy. He blames that on the beer he had the night before. Fortunately, Randall lives only five minutes from work. Despite this, he doesn't have enough time to take a shower. He grabs the same uniform he wore the day before when prepping chicken. He also puts on his watch and several rings.

Randall does not have luck on his side today. On the way to the restaurant, his oil light comes on. He is forced to pull off the road and add oil to his car. When he gets to work, he realizes that he has left his hat at home. Randall is greeted by an angry manager. The manager puts Randall to work right away, loading the rotisserie with raw chicken. Randall then moves to serving a customer who orders a freshly made salad. Randall is known for his salads and makes the salad to the customer's approval.

The manager asks Randall to take out the garbage and then make potato salad for the lunch hour rush. On the way back from the garbage run, Randall tells the manager that his stomach is bothering him. The manager, thinking of his staff shortage, asks Randall to stick it out as long as he can. Randall agrees and gets out the ingredients for the potato salad. Then he heads to the restroom in hope of relieving his symptoms. After quickly rinsing his hands in the restroom, he finds that the paper towels have run out. Short of time, he wipes his hands on his apron.

The manager tells Randall to clean the few tables in the deli that are available for customers. When finished, Randall grabs a piece of chicken from the rotisserie for a snack. He takes the chicken with him to the prep area, so he can get back to making the potato salad.

Randall and his manager made several errors. Identify as many as you can on a separate piece of paper.

For answers, please turn to page 3.21.

Study Questions

Circle the best answer to each question.

① **After which activity must food handlers wash their hands?**

A Putting on gloves

B Serving customers

C Applying hand antiseptic

D Clearing tables

② **What should food handlers do after prepping food and before using the restroom?**

A Wash their hands

B Take off their hats

C Change their gloves

D Take off their aprons

③ **Which piece of jewelry can be worn on a food handler's hand or arm?**

A Watch

B Diamond ring

C Plain band ring

D Medical bracelet

④ **When should hand antiseptics be used?**

A After washing hands

B Before washing hands

C When soap is unavailable

D When gloves are not being used

⑤ **A food handler will be wearing single-use gloves to chop lettuce for an hour. When must the food handler's hands be washed?**

A After putting on the gloves

B Before starting the task

C Half-way through the task

D Each time gloves are changed

⑥ **A cook wore single-use gloves while forming raw ground beef into patties. The cook continued to wear them while slicing hamburger buns. What mistake was made?**

A The cook did not wear reusable gloves while handling the raw ground beef and hamburger buns.

B The cook did not clean and sanitize the gloves before handling the hamburger buns.

C The cook did not wash hands before putting on the same gloves to slice the hamburger buns.

D The cook did not wash hands and put on new gloves before slicing the hamburger buns.

⑦ **A food handler has diarrhea and has been diagnosed with an illness from** *Shigella* **spp. What should the manager tell this food handler to do?**

A Wear gloves while handling food.

B Work in a nonfood handling position

C Stay home until approved to return to work.

D Wash hands frequently while handling food.

⑧ **A food handler prepares and delivers meals to elderly individuals receiving cancer care services at home. What symptoms require this food handler to stay home from work?**

A Thirst with itching

B Soreness with fatigue

C Sore throat with fever

D Headache with soreness

⑨ **When is it acceptable to eat in an operation?**

A When prepping food

B When washing dishes

C When sitting in a break area

D When handling utensils

⑩ **What should a manager of a hospital cafeteria do if a cook calls in with a headache, nausea, and diarrhea?**

A Tell the cook to stay away from work and see a doctor.

B Tell the cook to come in for a couple of hours and then go home.

C Tell the cook to rest for a couple of hours and then come to work.

D Tell the cook to go to the doctor and then immediately come to work.

For answers, please turn to page 3.21.

Answers

3.3   Who Is at Risk?

1, 3, 5, 6, and 8 should be marked.

3.14   Check Your Handwashing Savvy

① E

② G

③ B

④ C

⑤ J

3.15   When to Wash Hands?

Paul should have washed his hands at the following times.

- Before getting the chicken from the cooler
- Before putting on the first pair of gloves
- After shaking hands with the owner and before putting on the second pair of gloves
- After finishing prepping the chicken
- After loading the dishes into the dishwasher
- Before putting on gloves and handling the vegetables for the salad bar
- After sneezing and before putting on the third pair of gloves
- After using the restroom
- Before putting on the fourth pair of gloves and continuing to prep vegetables
- Before working on the grill
- Before touching the raw chicken breast
- After placing the raw chicken breast on the grill and before handling the fresh bun

3.15   Exclusion or Restriction?

① R

② E

③ E

3.17   **Chapter Review Case Study**

Randall made the following errors.

- Randall did not take a bath or shower before work.
- Randall wore a dirty uniform to work.
- Randall should have removed his watch and rings (with the exception of a plain band) before prepping and serving food.
- Randall did not wear a hair restraint.
- Randall did not report his illness to the manager before coming to work.
- Randall did not wash his hands before handling the raw chicken.
- Randall did not wash his hands after handling the raw chicken.
- The manager did not ask about Randall's symptoms. If Randall were to report that he had diarrhea, the manager should have sent him home.
- Randall did not wash his hands correctly after taking out the garbage.
- Randall did not wash his hands correctly after using the restroom.
- Randall did not dry his hands correctly after washing them. He got them dirty again when he wiped them on his apron.
- Randall wore his apron into the restroom.
- The manager did not make sure the restroom was stocked with paper towels.
- Randall touched the ready-to-eat chicken with his contaminated hands.
- Randall was eating chicken while prepping food.

3.18   **Study Questions**

1. D   6. D
2. D   7. C
3. C   8. C
4. A   9. C
5. B   10. A

chapter 4
The Flow of Food: An Introduction

Hazards in the Flow of Food	Monitoring Time and Temperature	
— The Flow of Food — Cross-Contamination — Time-Temperature Control	— Bimetallic Stemmed Thermometer — Thermocouples and Thermistors — Infrared (Laser) Thermometers	— Other Temperature-Recording Devices — General Thermometer Guidelines

(((NEWS))) University Outbreak

An outbreak of *Salmonella* sickened 32 visitors to a university located in the northeastern United States. The sickened guests had attended a luncheon hosted by the chancellor during graduation weekend. Reports of illness flooded the local media, the university's on-campus clinic, and the local regulatory authority. Symptoms included stomach pain, nausea, diarrhea, chills, and vomiting.

It was determined that a new food handler at the dining facility had cross-contaminated romaine lettuce used for a chicken Caesar salad served at the luncheon. In her haste to catch up during a busy shift, the food handler chopped the lettuce on a cutting board that had been used to prep raw chicken for the salad. The cutting board had not been cleaned and sanitized between uses.

The university's contractor for foodservice announced that they would work closely with the local inspector to correct the problem. They would also immediately implement a program that would prevent cross-contamination in the future.

You Can Prevent This

As you can see in the story above, preventing cross-contamination is critical for keeping food safe. But you must also control time and temperature when handling food. In this chapter, you will learn about the following tools and practices to help you keep food safe.

- Preventing cross-contamination
- Preventing time-temperature abuse
- Using the correct kinds of thermometers to take temperatures

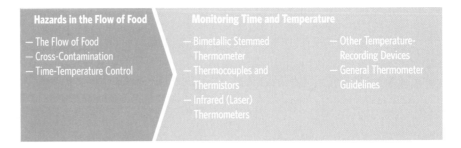

Hazards in the Flow of Food	Monitoring Time and Temperature	
— The Flow of Food	— Bimetallic Stemmed Thermometer	— Other Temperature-Recording Devices
— Cross-Contamination	— Thermocouples and Thermistors	— General Thermometer Guidelines
— Time-Temperature Control	— Infrared (Laser) Thermometers	

Hazards in the Flow of Food

To keep food safe, you must apply what you learn in the ServSafe program throughout the flow of food. This requires a good understanding of how to prevent cross-contamination and time-temperature abuse.

The Flow of Food

The path that food takes through your operation is called the flow of food. It begins when you buy the food and ends when you serve it.

💲	Purchasing	chapter 5
🚚	Receiving	chapter 5
🚪	Storing	chapter 5
🔪	Preparation	chapter 6
	Cooking	chapter 6
🕐	Holding	chapter 7
❄️	Cooling	chapter 6
	Reheating	chapter 6
🍽️	Serving	chapter 7

You are responsible for the safety of the food at every point in this flow—and many things can happen to it.

For example, a frozen food might be safe when it leaves the processor's plant. However, on the way to the supplier's warehouse, the food might thaw. Once in your operation, the food might not be stored correctly, or it might not be cooked to the correct internal temperature. These mistakes can add up and cause a foodborne illness.

Cross-Contamination

Pathogens can move around easily in your operation. They can be spread from food or unwashed hands to prep areas, equipment, utensils, or other food.

Cross-contamination can happen at almost any point in the flow of food. When you know how and where it can happen, it is fairly easy to prevent. The most basic way is to keep raw and ready-to-eat food away from each other.

Here are some guidelines for doing this.

Using separate equipment   Each type of food should have separate equipment. For example, use one set of cutting boards, utensils, and containers for raw poultry. Use another set for raw meat. Use a third set for produce. Colored cutting boards and utensil handles can help keep equipment separate. The color tells food handlers which equipment to use with each food item. You might use yellow for raw chicken, red for raw meat, and green for produce, as the prep chef is doing in the photo at left.

Cleaning and sanitizing   Clean and sanitize all work surfaces, equipment, and utensils after each task. When you cut up raw chicken, for example, you cannot get by with just rinsing the equipment. Pathogens such as nontyphoidal *Salmonella* can contaminate food through cross-contamination. To prevent this, you must wash, rinse, and sanitize equipment. See chapter 10 for more information on cleaning and sanitizing.

Prepping food at different times   If you need to use the same table to prep different types of food, prep raw meat, fish, and poultry; and ready-to-eat food at different times. You must clean and sanitize work surfaces and utensils between each type of food. For example, by prepping ready-to-eat food before raw food, you can minimize the chance for cross-contamination.

Buying prepared food   Buy food that doesn't require much prepping or handling. For example, you could buy precooked chicken breasts or chopped lettuce, as shown in the photo at left.

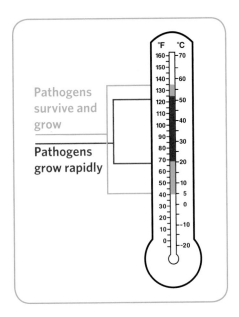

Pathogens survive and grow

Pathogens grow rapidly

Time-Temperature Control

Most foodborne illnesses happen because TCS food has been time-temperature abused. Remember, TCS food has been time-temperature abused any time it remains between 41°F and 135°F (5°C and 57°C). This is called the temperature danger zone because pathogens grow in this range. But most pathogens grow much faster between 70°F and 125°F (21°C and 52°C). These ranges are shown at left. Food is being temperature abused whenever it is handled in the following ways.

- Cooked to the wrong internal temperature
- Held at the wrong temperature
- Cooled or reheated incorrectly

The longer food stays in the temperature danger zone, the more time pathogens have to grow. To keep food safe, you must reduce the time it spends in this temperature range. If food is held in this range for four or more hours, you must throw it out.

Avoiding Time-Temperature Abuse

Food handlers should avoid time-temperature abuse by following good policies and procedures.

Monitoring   Learn which food items should be checked, how often, and by whom. Make sure food handlers understand what to do, how to do it, and why it is important. For example, the manager in the photo at left is making sure the cook can check the temperature of a chicken breast.

Tools   Make sure the correct kinds of thermometers are available. Give food handlers their own thermometers. Have them use timers in prep areas to check how long food is in the temperature danger zone.

Recording   Have food handlers record temperatures regularly, as the chef is doing in the photo at left. Make sure they write down when the temperatures were taken. Print simple forms for recording this information. Post them on clipboards outside of coolers and freezers, near prep areas, and next to cooking and holding equipment.

Time and temperature control   Have procedures to limit the time food spends in the temperature danger zone. This might include limiting the amount of food that can be removed from a cooler when prepping it.

Corrective actions   Make sure food handlers know what to do when time and temperature standards are not met. For example, if you hold soup on a steam table and its temperature falls below 135°F (57°C) after two hours, you might reheat it to the correct temperature or throw it out.

Apply Your Knowledge

An Ounce of Prevention

Write an ✘ next to the practice if it helps prevent cross-contamination.

① _____ Use separate cutting boards for prepping raw meat and raw vegetables.

② _____ Wash and rinse a cutting board after prepping raw fish.

③ _____ Buy diced onions instead of dicing them in the operation.

④ _____ Prep salads before prepping raw meat on the same prep table.

⑤ _____ Use green-handled knives to prep produce and yellow-handled knives to prep raw poultry.

⑥ _____ Wipe down prep tables with a wiping cloth between different tasks.

⑦ _____ Cook chicken in-house instead of buying precooked chicken.

Is It Safe?

Read each story and decide if the food handler handled the food safely. Explain why or why not in the space provided.

Anita had to prepare 6 tuna salad sandwiches. She went to the cooler and pulled out a large hotel pan of tuna salad and put it on the prep table. She was interrupted several times to help with other tasks. After assembling the sandwiches, she covered the pan of tuna salad, dated it, and put it back in the cooler.

① Did Anita handle the food safely? Why or why not?

_____

_____

_____

_____

_____

_____

Jerry cut up raw chickens on a cutting board on the prep table. Then he washed and rinsed the table and equipment he used. After that, he sliced onions and peppers on the same cutting board on the prep table. Before he left for the day, he washed, rinsed, and sanitized the prep table and equipment.

② Did Jerry handle the food safely? Why or why not?

_____

_____

_____

_____

_____

_____

For answers, please turn to page 4.14.

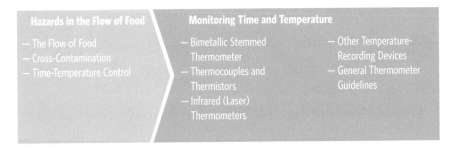

Hazards in the Flow of Food	Monitoring Time and Temperature	

— The Flow of Food
— Cross-Contamination
— Time-Temperature Control
	— Bimetallic Stemmed
	  Thermometer
	— Thermocouples and
	  Thermistors
	— Infrared (Laser)
	  Thermometers
		— Other Temperature-
		  Recording Devices
		— General Thermometer
		  Guidelines

Monitoring Time and Temperature

To keep food safe, you must control the amount of time it spends in the temperature danger zone. This requires monitoring. The most important tool you have to monitor temperature is the thermometer. Three types are commonly used in operations.

- Bimetallic stemmed thermometers

- Thermocouples

- Thermistors

Bimetallic Stemmed Thermometer

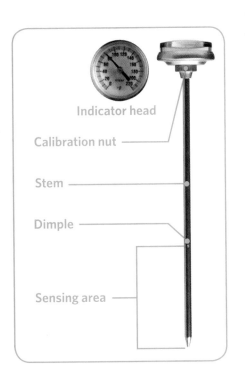

Indicator head

Calibration nut

Stem

Dimple

Sensing area

A bimetallic stemmed thermometer, shown in the photo at left, can check temperatures from 0°F to 220°F (–18°C to 104°C). This makes it useful for checking temperatures during the flow of food. For example, you can use it to check food temperatures during receiving. You can also use it to check food in a hot- or cold-holding unit.

A bimetallic stemmed thermometer measures temperature through its metal stem. When checking temperatures, insert the stem into the food up to the dimple. You must do this because the sensing area of the thermometer goes from the tip of the stem to the dimple. This trait makes this thermometer useful for checking the temperature of large or thick food. It is usually not practical for thin food, such as hamburger patties.

If you buy these thermometers for your operation, make sure they have these features.

Calibration nut   You can adjust the thermometer to make it accurate by using its calibration nut.

Easy-to-read markings   Clear markings reduce the chance that someone will misread the thermometer. The thermometer must be scaled in at least two-degree increments.

Dimple   The dimple is the mark on the stem that shows the end of the temperature-sensing area.

Thermocouples and Thermistors

Thermocouples, such as the one in the photo at left, and thermistors are also common in operations. They measure temperatures through a metal probe. Temperatures are displayed digitally. The sensing area on thermocouples and thermistors is on the tip of their probe. This means you don't have to insert them into the food as far as bimetallic stemmed thermometers to get a correct reading. Thermocouples and thermistors are good for checking the temperature of both thick and thin food.

Thermocouples and thermistors come in several styles and sizes. Many come with different types of probes. The photos below show some basic types.

Immersion probes   Use these to check the temperature of liquids. This could include soups, sauces, and frying oil.

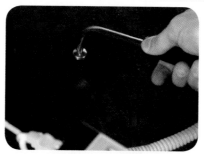

Surface probes   Use these to check the temperature of flat cooking equipment, such as griddles.

Penetration probes   Use these to check the internal temperature of food. They are especially useful for checking the temperatures of thin food, such as hamburger patties or fish fillets.

Air probes   Use these to check the temperature inside coolers and ovens.

Infrared (Laser) Thermometers

Infrared thermometers measure the temperatures of food and equipment surfaces. For example, the food handler in the photo at left is using one to measure the temperature of a grill top. These thermometers are quick and easy to use.

Infrared thermometers do not need to touch a surface to check its temperature. This means there is less chance for cross-contamination and damage to food. However, these thermometers cannot measure air temperature or the internal temperature of food.

Follow these guidelines for using infrared thermometers.

Distance   Hold the thermometer as close to the food or equipment as you can without touching it.

Barriers   Remove anything between the thermometer and the food, food package, or equipment. Do NOT take readings through metal, such as stainless steel or aluminum. Do NOT take readings through glass.

Manufacturer's directions   Always follow the manufacturer's guidelines. This should give you the most accurate readings.

Other Temperature-Recording Devices

Other tools are available that can help you monitor temperature. A maximum registering thermometer is one type. This thermometer indicates the highest temperature reached during use and is used where temperature readings cannot be continuously observed. It works well for checking final rinse temperatures of dishwashing machines.

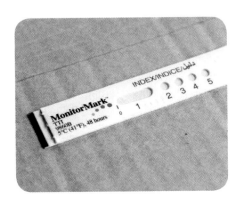

Some devices monitor both time and temperature. The time-temperature indicator (TTI), shown in the photo at left, is an example. These tags are attached to packaging by the supplier. A color change appears in the window if the food has been time-temperature abused during shipment or storage. This color change is not reversible, so you know if the food has been abused.

Some suppliers place temperature-recording devices inside their delivery trucks. These devices constantly check and record temperatures. You can check the device during receiving to make sure food was at safe temperatures while it was being shipped.

General Thermometer Guidelines

You should know how to use and care for each type of thermometer in your operation. In general, follow the guidelines below. However, you should always follow manufacturers' directions.

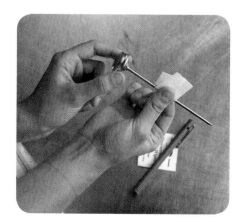

Cleaning and sanitizing   Thermometers must be washed, rinsed, sanitized, as seen in the photo at left, and air-dried. Keep storage cases clean, too. Do these things before and after using thermometers to prevent cross-contamination. Be sure the sanitizing solution you use is for food-contact surfaces. Always have plenty of clean and sanitized thermometers on hand.

Calibration   Thermometers can lose their accuracy when they are bumped or dropped. It can also happen when they go through severe temperature change. When this happens, the thermometer must be calibrated, or adjusted, to give a correct reading. Make sure your thermometers are accurate by calibrating them regularly. You should do this before each shift. You should also do this before the first delivery arrives. Some thermometers cannot be calibrated and must be replaced. Others will need to be sent back to the manufacturer for calibration. Follow the manufacturer's directions regarding calibration.

Accuracy   Thermometers used to measure the temperature of food must be accurate to +/- 2°F or +/- 1°C. Thermometers used to measure air temperature in food-storage equipment must be accurate to +/- 3°F or +/- 1.5°C. A hanging thermometer in a walk-in cooler is an example.

Glass thermometers   Glass thermometers, such as candy thermometers, can be a physical contaminant if they break. They can only be used when enclosed in a shatterproof casing.

Checking temperatures   When checking the temperature of food, insert the probe into the thickest part of the food, as shown in the photo at left. This is usually in the center. Also, take another reading in a different spot. The temperature may vary in different areas.

Before recording a temperature, wait for the thermometer reading to steady. While digital thermometers are capable of displaying the temperature instantly, bimetallic stemmed thermometers will take more time. Allow at least 15 seconds after you insert the thermometer stem into the food.

Apply Your Knowledge

Pick the Correct Thermometer

For each situation, choose the best thermometer or thermometers. Some thermometers may be chosen more than once. Write the letter or letters in the space provided.

① _____ Internal temperature of a chicken breast

② _____ Internal temperature of a roast

③ _____ Internal temperature of a large stockpot of soup

④ _____ Surface temperature of a grill

⑤ _____ Air temperature of a cooler

Ⓐ Bimetallic stemmed thermometer

Ⓑ Thermocouple with immersion probe

Ⓒ Thermocouple with surface probe

Ⓓ Thermocouple with penetration probe

Ⓔ Thermocouple with air probe

Ⓕ Infrared thermometer

For answers, please turn to page 4.14.

Summary

- The flow of food is the path food takes in your operation from purchasing to service. Many things can happen to food in its flow through the operation. Two major concerns are cross-contamination and time-temperature abuse.

- To prevent cross-contamination, use separate equipment for each type of food. Also, you must clean and sanitize all work surfaces, equipment, and utensils after each task. Prepping ready-to-eat food before raw meat, poultry, and fish is one way to minimize the chance for cross-contamination. Similarly, you can buy food items that don't require much preparation or handling.

- Time-temperature abuse happens any time food remains between 41°F and 135°F (5°C and 57°C). This range is called the temperature danger zone. You must try to keep food out of this range.

- A thermometer is the most important tool you can use to prevent time-temperature abuse. You should regularly record food temperatures and the times they were taken.

- Always put the thermometer stem or probe into the thickest part of the food. A bimetallic stemmed thermometer should be put into food from the tip to the end of the sensing area. Before you record the temperature, wait for the thermometer reading to steady. Never use glass thermometers with food items unless they are enclosed in a shatterproof casing.

- Thermometers should be calibrated regularly. Most important, they must be cleaned and sanitized before and after each use.

Chapter Review Case Study

To keep food safe, you must prevent cross-contamination; prevent time-temperature abuse; check food temperatures using the correct kinds of thermometers; and keep your thermometers accurate.

Now, take what you have learned in this chapter and apply it to the following case study.

At 6:00 a.m., Kim started her work day at The Little Bistro. After a quick meeting with the chef, her first task was to make the broccoli quiches for the lunch special. By 6:15, she had collected all the ingredients except the broccoli. She set salt, eggs, cream, butter, and cheese on the prep table by the mixer. On her last trip to the cooler, she got the broccoli. It took over an hour to wash and chop it. Finally, she was able to mix the quiche filling. She cracked eggs in a bowl. Then she added the remaining ingredients. She dripped egg whites on the table, making a mess. Leaving the leftover eggs and cream on the table, she got out the premade quiche crusts from the freezer and poured the filling. By the time she got the quiches in the oven, it was 10:30.

Kim hurried to start her next task—making fruit salad. First, she washed her hands and put on gloves. Then she quickly removed the rinds from some melons. She then sliced them on the salad-prep table. The juice made a mess, so she wiped the table. Kim took off her gloves and washed her hands. Before she could start on the other fruit, the oven timer went off.

Kim then checked the quiches. They were supposed to bake for around 30 minutes. However, she did not want to overcook them. The chef said their internal temperature needed to be 155°F (68°C). She used an infrared thermometer to check the temperature of one quiche in two places. The readings were in the correct range. She took the quiches out of the oven and set them on a table to cool. While they cooled, Kim went back to the fruit salad. She washed her hands and put on gloves. Then she hurried to prep the strawberries, kiwi, and grapes on the same table as the melons. When she headed back to the cooler to get the citrus dressing for the salad, she noticed the eggs and cream she left out.

At 11:45, the lunch rush was in full swing. She grabbed the eggs on her way back to the cooler and put them away. After adding the dressing to the salad, she put the salad and the dressing in the cooler. Then she wiped the prep table and put away the leftover cream. After the rush, Kim cleaned and sanitized the mixer and both of the tables she used.

What did Kim do wrong?

For answers, please turn to page 4.14.

Study Questions

Circle the best answer to each question.

1. A food handler has finished trimming raw chicken on a cutting board and needs the board to prep vegetables. What must be done to the cutting board?

   A It must be dried with a paper towel.

   B It must be turned over to the other side.

   C It must be washed, rinsed, and sanitized.

   D It must be rinsed in hot water and air-dried.

2. How far must a bimetallic stemmed thermometer be inserted into food to give an accurate reading?

   A Up to the tip of the thermometer stem

   B Just past the tip of the thermometer stem

   C Past the dimple of the thermometer stem

   D Up to the dimple in the thermometer stem

3. Which probe should be used to check the temperature of a large stockpot of chili?

   A Air probe

   B Immersion probe

   C Penetration probe

   D Surface probe

4. At what temperatures do most foodborne pathogens grow most quickly?

   A Between 0°F and 41°F (-17°C and 5°C)

   B Between 45°F and 65°F (7°C and 18°C)

   C Between 70°F and 125°F (21°C and 52°C)

   D Between 130°F and 165°F (54°C and 74°C)

5. Which type of thermometer can read temperature without touching the item's surface?

   A Air probe

   B Immersion probe

   C Infrared

   D TTI

⑥ **A thermometer used to measure the temperature of food must be accurate to what temperature?**

   A   +/- 2°F or +/- 1°C

   B   +/- 4°F or +/- 3°C

   C   +/- 6°F or +/- 5°C

   D   +/- 8°F or +/- 7°C

⑦ **What device can be used to record time-temperature abuse during the delivery of food?**

   A   Bimetallic stemmed thermometer

   B   Thermistor

   C   Thermocouple

   D   Time-temperature indicator

For answers, please turn to page 4.14.

Answers

4.5   An Ounce of Prevention

1, 3, 4, and 5 should be marked.

4.5   Is It Safe?

① No. Anita took out more tuna salad than she needed to make a small number of sandwiches. This exposed the tuna salad to time-temperature abuse, which was made worse by the many interruptions.

② No. Jerry did not sanitize the table and equipment after he cut up the chickens. The onions and peppers could have been contaminated by the chickens.

4.10   Pick the Correct Thermometer

① A, D

② A, D

③ B

④ C, F

⑤ E

4.11   Chapter Review Case Study

Kim did the following things wrong.

- She left the eggs and dairy at room temperature for too long. The quiche filling was at room temperature for four hours and 15 minutes. The leftover eggs and dairy were at room temperature for five and a half hours. She should have thrown away the leftover egg and dairy.

- She used the wrong kind of thermometer to check the internal temperature of the quiches.

- She let the quiches cool at room temperature and did not store them correctly.

- She did not clean and sanitize the prep table by the mixer after she finished preparing the quiches.

- She did not clean and sanitize the salad prep table after she cut the melons and before prepping the other fruit.

- She should have washed her hands before making the quiches.

4.12   Study Questions

① C   ⑤ C

② D   ⑥ A

③ B   ⑦ D

④ C

Notes

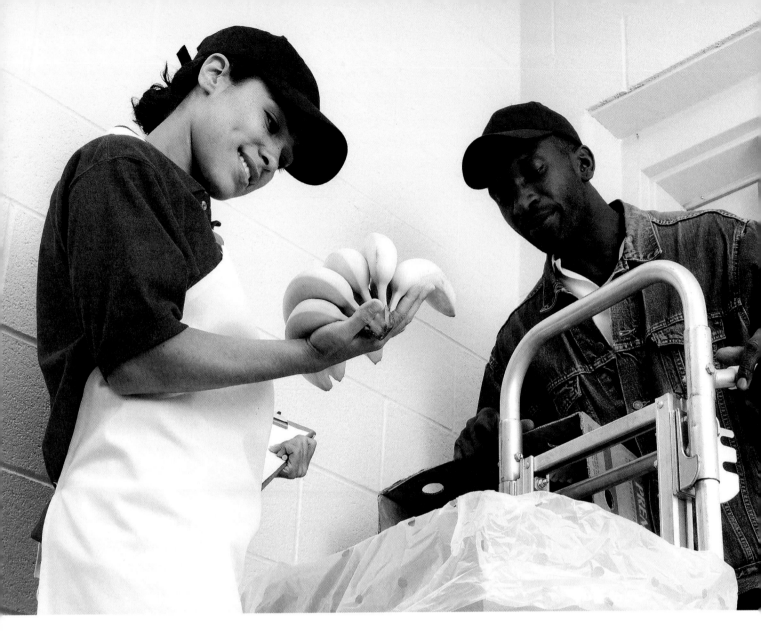

chapter 5
The Flow of Food: Purchasing, Receiving, and Storage

Fatal Outbreak Linked to Incorrect Storage Practices

Two deaths and 68 cases of severe illness were attributed to an *E. coli* outbreak at a local family operation in the Midwest. An investigation revealed that several 10-pound packages of raw ground beef were incorrectly stored on the top shelf in a walk-in cooler. Authorities determined that the ground beef dripped onto fresh rolls and cartons of chocolate milk that were stored on the shelf below. Guests who had eaten the rolls or were served the cartons of chocolate milk got sick. The operation, which had voluntarily closed for the investigation, never reopened.

You Can Prevent This

In the story above, incorrect storage practices led to contaminated food. Unfortunately, the problem was not found in time to prevent the tragedy.

In this chapter, you will learn about storage practices that can help prevent this type of situation. You will also learn about practices that can be put in place to help ensure the food you receive is safe.

* Purchasing food from approved, reputable suppliers
* Using criteria to accept or reject food during receiving
* Labeling and dating food
* Storing food and nonfood items to prevent time-temperature abuse and contamination

General Purchasing and Receiving Principles	Storing
— Purchasing — Receiving and Inspecting	— Labeling — Date Marking — Temperatures — Rotation — Preventing Cross-Contamination

General Purchasing and Receiving Principles

You can't make unsafe food safe. So, you must make sure you bring only safe food into your operation. Purchasing food from approved, reputable suppliers, and following good receiving procedures will help to ensure the safety and quality of the food your operation uses.

Purchasing

Before you accept any deliveries, you must make sure that the food you purchase is safe. Follow these guidelines.

Photo courtesy of Boskovich Farms, Inc.

Approved, reputable suppliers   Food must be purchased from approved, reputable suppliers. These suppliers have been inspected and can show you an inspection report. They also meet all applicable local, state, and federal laws. This applies to all suppliers in the supply chain. Your operation's chain can include growers (as shown in the photo at left), shippers, packers, manufacturers, distributors (trucking fleets and warehouses), and local markets.

Develop a relationship with your suppliers, and get to know their food safety practices. Consider reviewing their most recent inspection reports. These reports can be from the U.S. Department of Agriculture (USDA), the Food and Drug Administration (FDA), or a third-party inspector. They should be based on Good Manufacturing Practices (GMP) or Good Agricultural Practices (GAP). Make sure the inspection report reviews the following areas.

- Receiving and storage
- Processing
- Shipping
- Cleaning and sanitizing
- Personal hygiene
- Staff training
- Recall program
- HACCP program or other food safety system

Many operations establish supplier lists based on their company specifications, standards, and procedures. However, only approved suppliers should be included on these lists.

Deliveries   Suppliers must deliver food when staff has enough time to do inspections. Schedule deliveries at a time when they can be correctly received.

Receiving and Inspecting

You must take steps to ensure the receiving and inspection process is smooth and safe. Make specific staff responsible for receiving. Train them to follow food safety guidelines. In the photo at left, a manager is training a food handler on inspecting produce. Provide staff with the tools they need, including purchase orders, thermometers, and scales. Then make sure enough trained staff are available to receive and inspect food items promptly. This starts by visually inspecting delivery trucks for signs of contamination. It continues with visually inspecting the food items and checking to make sure they have been received at the correct temperature. Once inspected, food items must be stored as quickly as possible in the correct areas. This is especially true for refrigerated and frozen items.

Key Drop Deliveries

Some foodservice operations receive food after-hours when they are closed for business. This is often referred to as a key drop delivery. The supplier is given a key or other access to the operation to make the delivery. Products are then placed in coolers, freezers, and dry-storage areas. The delivery must be inspected once you arrive at the operation and must meet the following conditions.

- It is from an approved source.
- It was placed in the correct storage location to maintain the required temperature.
- It was protected from contamination in storage.
- It has not been contaminated.
- It is honestly presented.

Rejecting Items

If you must reject an item, set it aside from the items you are accepting. Then tell the delivery person exactly what's wrong with the rejected item. Make sure you get a signed adjustment or credit slip before giving the item back to the delivery person. Finally, log the incident on the invoice or the receiving document.

Occasionally, you may be able to recondition and use items that would have been rejected. For example, a shipment of cans with contaminated surfaces may be cleaned and sanitized, allowing them to be used. However, the same cans may not be reconditioned if they are damaged.

Recalls

Food items you have received may sometimes be recalled by the manufacturer. This may happen when food contamination is confirmed or suspected. It can also occur when items have been mislabeled or misbranded. Often food is recalled when food allergens have not been identified on the label. Most vendors will notify you of the recall. However, you should also monitor recall notifications made by the FDA and the USDA. Follow these guidelines when notified of a recall.

- Identify the recalled food items by matching information from the recall notice to the item. This may include the manufacturer's ID, the time the item was manufactured, and the item's use-by date.

- Remove the item from inventory, and place it in a secure and appropriate location. That may be a cooler or dry-storage area. The recalled item must be stored separately from food, utensils, equipment, linens, and single-use items.

- Label the item in a way that will prevent it from being placed back in inventory. Some operations do this by including a Do Not Use and Do Not Discard label on recalled food items. Inform staff not to use the product.

- Refer to the vendor's notification or recall notice for what to do with the item. For example, you might be instructed to throw it out or return it to the vendor.

Temperature

Use thermometers to check food temperatures during receiving. The following examples explain how to check the temperatures of various types of food.

Checking the Temperature of Various Types of Food

Meat, poultry, and fish Insert the thermometer stem or probe directly into the thickest part of the food. The center is usually the thickest part.

ROP food (MAP, vacuum-packed, and *sous vide* food) Insert the thermometer stem or probe between two packages. If the package allows, fold it around the thermometer stem or probe. Be careful **NOT** to puncture the package.

Other packaged food Open the package and insert the thermometer stem or probe into the food. The sensing area must be fully immersed in the food. The stem or probe must **NOT** touch the package.

Deliveries should also meet the following temperature criteria.

Cold food   Receive cold TCS food, such as the fish in the photo at left, at 41°F (5°C) or lower, unless otherwise specified.

Live shellfish   Receive oysters, mussels, clams, and scallops at an air temperature of 45°F (7°C) and an internal temperature no greater than 50°F (10°C). Once received, the shellfish must be cooled to 41°F (5°C) or lower in four hours.

Shucked shellfish   Receive at 45°F (7°C) or lower. Cool the shellfish to 41°F (5°C) or lower in four hours.

Milk   Receive at 45°F (7°C) or lower. Cool the milk to 41°F (5°C) or lower in four hours.

Shell eggs   Receive at an air temperature of 45°F (7°C) or lower.

Hot food   Receive hot TCS food at 135°F (57°C) or higher.

Frozen food   Frozen food should be frozen solid when received.

Reject frozen food for the following reasons.

- Fluids or water stains appear in case bottoms or on packaging.

- There are ice crystals or frozen liquids on the food or the packaging. This may be evidence of thawing and refreezing, which shows the food has been time-temperature abused. The food in the photo at left shows evidence of thawing and refreezing.

Packaging

Both food items and nonfood items such as single-use cups, utensils, and napkins, must be packaged correctly when you receive them. Items should be delivered in their original packaging with a manufacturer's label. The packaging should be intact, clean, and protect food and food-contact surfaces from contamination. Reject food and nonfood items if packaging has any of the following problems.

Damage   Reject items with tears, holes, or punctures in their packaging. Likewise, reject cans with labels that are not intact or have bulging or swollen ends, rust, or dents. All food packaged in a reduced-oxygen environment, such as vacuum-packed meat, must be rejected if the packaging is bloated or leaking. Items with broken cartons or seals, or items with dirty and discolored packaging should also be rejected. Do NOT accept cases or packages that appear to have been tampered with.

Liquid   Reject items with leaks, dampness, or water stains (which means the item was wet at some point), as shown in the photo at left.

Pests   Reject items with signs of pests or pest damage.

Dates   Food items must be correctly labeled. Do NOT accept food that is missing use-by or expiration dates from the manufacturer. Reject items that have passed their use-by or expiration dates. Some operations label food items with the date the item was received to help with stock rotation during storage.

Documents

Food items must be delivered with the correct documents. For example, shellfish must be received with shellstock identification tags. These tags indicate when and where the shellfish were harvested. They must be kept on file for 90 days from the date the last shellfish was used from its delivery container.

Fish that will be eaten raw or partially cooked must also be received with the correct documentation. These documents must indicate the fish was correctly frozen before you received it. Keep these documents for 90 days from the sale of the fish. If the fish was farm raised, it must have documentation that states the fish was raised to FDA standards. These documents must also be kept for 90 days from the sale of the fish.

Food Quality

Poor food quality can be a sign that the food has been time-temperature abused and, therefore, may be unsafe. Work with your suppliers to define specific safety and quality criteria for the food items you typically receive. Reject food if it has any of the following problems.

Appearance   Reject food that is moldy or has an abnormal color. Food that is moist when it should be dry, such as salami, should also be rejected. Do not accept any food item that shows signs of pests or pest damage.

Texture   Reject meat, fish, or poultry that is slimy, sticky, or dry. Also reject it if it has soft flesh that leaves an imprint when you touch it.

Odor   Reject food with an abnormal or unpleasant odor.

In addition to the guidelines above, you should always reject any item that does not meet your company's standards for quality.

Apply Your Knowledge

Accept or Reject?

Write an A next to the food items you should accept. Write an R next to the food items you should reject.

① _____ Chicken received at an internal temperature of 50°F (10°C)

② _____ Can of red kidney beans with a small dent on one side of the can

③ _____ Shell eggs received at an air temperature of 45°F (7°C)

④ _____ Fresh salmon with flesh that springs back when touched

⑤ _____ Bag of flour that is dry but has a watermark on it

⑥ _____ Live oysters without shellstock identification tags

⑦ _____ Frozen meat with large ice crystals on the packaging

⑧ _____ Milk received at 50°F (10°C)

⑨ _____ Mozzarella cheese with small spots of mold

⑩ _____ Vacuum-packed bacon with the seal broken but no other obvious damage

For answers, please turn to page 5.18.

Storing

Following good storage guidelines for food and nonfood items will help keep these items safe and preserve their quality. In general, you must label and date mark your food correctly. You must also rotate food and store it at the correct temperature. Finally, you need to store items in a way that prevents cross-contamination.

Labeling

Labeling food is important for many reasons. Illnesses have occurred when unlabeled chemicals were mistaken for food such as flour, sugar, and baking powder.

Customers have also suffered allergic reactions when food was unknowingly prepped with a food allergen that was not labeled.

Labeling Food for Use On-site

- All items that are not in their original containers must be labeled.

- Food labels should include the common name of the food or a statement that clearly and accurately identifies it, as shown in the photo at left.

- It is not necessary to label food if it clearly will not be mistaken for another item. The food must be easily identified by sight.

Labeling Food That Is Packaged On-site for Retail Sale

Food packaged in the operation that is being sold to customers for use at home, such as bottled salad dressing, must be labeled. The label must include the following information.

- Common name of the food or a statement that clearly identifies it.

- Quantity of the food.

- List of ingredients and sub ingredients in descending order by weight. This is necessary if the item contains two or more ingredients.

- List of artificial colors and flavors in the food. Chemical preservatives must also be listed.

- Name and place of business of the manufacturer, packer, or distributor.

- Source of each major food allergen contained in the food. This is not necessary if the source is already part of the common name of the ingredient.

These labeling requirements do not apply to customers' leftover food items placed in carry-out containers.

Date Marking

Refrigeration slows the growth of most bacteria. Some types, such as *Listeria monocytogenes,* grow well at refrigeration temperatures. When food is refrigerated for long periods of time, these bacteria can grow enough to cause illness. For this reason, ready-to-eat TCS food must be marked if held for longer than 24 hours. It must indicate when the food must be sold, eaten, or thrown out.

Ready-to-eat TCS food can be stored for only seven days if it is held at 41°F (5°C) or lower. The count begins on the day that the food was prepared or a commercial container was opened. For example, a food handler that prepared and stored potato salad on October 1 would write a discard date of October 7 on the label.

Operations have a variety of systems for date marking. Some write the day or date the food was prepped on the label. Others write the use-by day or date on the label, as shown in the photo at left.

Sometimes, commercially processed food will have a use-by date that is less than seven days from the date the container was opened. In this case, the container should be marked with this use-by date as long as the date is based on food safety.

When combining food in a dish with different use-by dates, the discard date of the dish should be based on the earliest prepared food.

Here is an example: a food handler is prepping a jambalaya on December 4 using shrimp and sausage. The shrimp has a use-by date of December 8, and the sausage has a use-by date of December 10. So, the use-by date of the jambalaya is December 8.

Temperatures

Pathogens can grow when food is not stored at the correct temperature. Follow these guidelines to keep food safe.

- Store TCS food at an internal temperature of 41°F (5°C) or lower or 135°F (57°C) or higher.

- Store frozen food at temperatures that keep it frozen.

- Make sure storage units have at least one air temperature measuring device. It must be accurate to +/- 3°F or +/- 1.5°C. This device must be located in the warmest part of refrigerated units, and the coldest part of hot-holding units. The hanging thermometer in the photo at left is a common type of temperature measuring device used in coolers.

- Do not overload coolers or freezers. Storing too many food items prevents good airflow and makes the units work harder to stay cold. Be aware that frequent opening of the cooler lets warm air inside, which can affect food safety.

- Use open shelving. Do not line shelves with aluminum foil, sheet pans, or paper. This restricts circulation of cold air in the unit.

- Monitor food temperatures regularly. Randomly sample the temperature of stored food to verify that the cooler is working.

Rotation

Food must be rotated in storage to maintain quality and limit the growth of pathogens. Food items must be rotated so that those with the earliest use-by or expiration dates are used before items with later dates.

Many operations use the first-in, first-out (FIFO) method to rotate their refrigerated, frozen, and dry food during storage. Here is one way to use the FIFO method.

❶ Identify the food item's use-by or expiration date.

❷ Store items with the earliest use-by or expiration dates in front of items with later dates, as shown in the photo at left.

❸ Once shelved, use those items stored in front first.

❹ Throw out food that has passed its manufacturer's use-by or expiration date.

Preventing Cross-Contamination

Food must be stored in ways that prevent cross-contamination. Follow the guidelines throughout this section.

Supplies

- Store all items in designated storage areas.
- Store items away from walls and at least six inches (15 centimeters) off the floor, as shown in the photo at left.
- Store single-use items (e.g., sleeve of single-use cups, single-use gloves) in original packaging.

6" (15 cm)

Containers

- Store food in containers intended for food.
- Use containers that are durable, leak proof, and able to be sealed or covered.
- NEVER use empty food containers to store chemicals. NEVER put food in empty chemical containers.

Cleaning

Keep all storage areas clean and dry. Clean floors, walls, and shelving in coolers, freezers, dry-storage areas, and heated holding cabinets on a regular basis, as shown in the photo at left. Clean up spills and leaks promptly to keep them from contaminating other food.

- Clean dollies, carts, transporters, and trays often.
- Store food in containers that have been cleaned and sanitized.
- Store dirty linens away from food. Store them in clean, nonabsorbent containers. They can also be stored in washable laundry bags.

Storage Order

- Wrap or cover food. Store raw meat, poultry, and seafood separately from ready-to-eat food. If raw and ready-to-eat food cannot be stored separately, store ready-to-eat food above raw meat, poultry, and seafood, as shown in the photo below. This will prevent juices from raw food from dripping onto ready-to-eat food.

- Raw meat, poultry, and seafood can be stored with or above ready-to-eat food in a freezer if all of the items have been commercially processed and packaged. Frozen food that is being thawed in coolers must also be stored below ready-to-eat food.

- Store raw meat, poultry, and seafood in coolers in the following top-to-bottom order: seafood, whole cuts of beef and pork, ground meat and ground fish, whole and ground poultry. This order is based on the minimum internal cooking temperature of each food. As an exception, ground meat and ground fish can be stored above whole cuts of beef and pork. To do this, make sure the packaging keeps out pathogens and chemicals. It also must not leak.

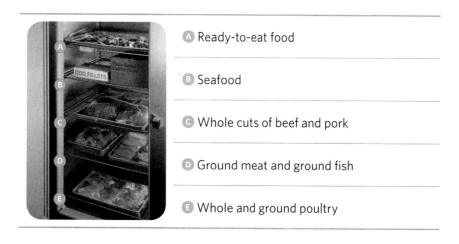

- Ⓐ Ready-to-eat food

- Ⓑ Seafood

- Ⓒ Whole cuts of beef and pork

- Ⓓ Ground meat and ground fish

- Ⓔ Whole and ground poultry

Storage Location

Food should be stored in a clean, dry location away from dust and other contaminants. **NEVER** store food in these areas to prevent contamination.

- Locker rooms or dressing rooms

- Restroom or garbage rooms

- Mechanical rooms

- Under unshielded sewer lines or leaking water lines

- Under stairwells

Apply Your Knowledge

Load the Cooler

Next to the number of each food item, write the letter of the shelf it belongs on.

① _____ Whole meat

② _____ Whole chicken

③ _____ Pecan pie

④ _____ Raw ground beef

(raw fish image)

⑤ _____ Raw fish

What's Wrong with This Picture?

Find the unsafe storage practices in this picture.

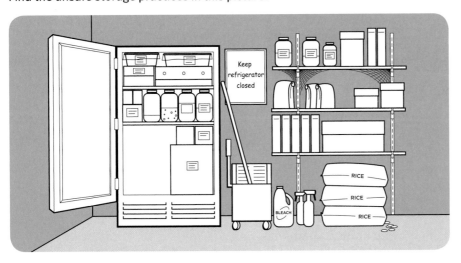

_____

_____

_____

For answers, please turn to page 5.18.

Chapter Summary

- Food must be purchased from approved, reputable suppliers. These suppliers must be inspected and meet applicable local, state, and federal laws.

- Deliveries must be inspected by designated staff trained to follow food safety guidelines. That will include a visual inspection of food as well as checks to make sure the food has been received at the correct temperature.

- Sometimes food items will be recalled by the manufacturer. Identify these items, remove them from inventory, and secure them in an appropriate location. Mark them so that staff does not use them.

- Cold TCS food must be received at 41°F (5°C) or lower. Hot TCS food must be received at 135°F (57°C) or higher. Frozen food should always be received frozen. Some items have other temperature requirements. Received food should have the correct color, texture, and odor.

- The packaging of delivered food items must be intact and clean, and it must protect food from contamination. There should also be no signs of pests or dampness. Food items should be correctly labeled and contain the correct documentation.

- Food must be stored in ways that prevent cross-contamination. Raw meat, poultry, and seafood should be stored separately from ready-to-eat food. If this is not possible, store ready-to-eat food above raw meat, poultry, and seafood.

- Food should be labeled before it is stored. The label should include the common name of the food. If TCS food was prepped in-house and will be stored longer than 24 hours, it must also be date marked. This food can be stored for only seven days if held at 41°F (5°C) or lower.

- Food should only be stored in a designated storage area. It should be stored away from walls and at least six inches (15 centimeters) off the floor. Stored food items should always be rotated so that older items are used first.

Chapter Review Case Study

To keep food safe during purchasing, receiving, and storage, you must know how to purchase food from approved, reputable suppliers; use criteria to accept and reject food during receiving; label and date food; and store food and nonfood items to prevent time-temperature abuse and contamination.

Now, take what you have learned in this chapter and apply it to the following case study.

A shipment was delivered to Enrico's Italian Restaurant on a warm summer day. Alyce, who was in charge of receiving, began inspecting the shipment. First, she inspected the bags of frozen shrimp. Alyce noticed the ice crystals inside the bags and took that as a good sign that the shrimp were still frozen.

Next she used a thermometer to test the temperature of the vacuum-packed packages of ground beef, which was 40°F (4°C). Then Alyce used the same thermometer to measure the temperature of the fresh salmon. The salmon was on ice, although it seemed as though much of the ice had melted. The internal temperature of the salmon was 43°F (6°C), and the flesh sprung back after she touched it. She accepted the ground beef and the salmon and put them on the side to put away.

Not wanting to take the time to clean and sanitize the probe, Alyce felt several containers of sour cream. They felt cold, so Alyce also put them on the side to put away. Finally, Alyce inspected the cases of pasta. One of the cases was torn, but the pasta inside the case didn't seem to be damaged.

Once she finished receiving the food, Alyce was ready to put it into storage. First, she carried the bags of shrimp to the freezer. She wondered who had left the freezer without making sure the door was completely shut. Alyce then loaded a case of sour cream on the dolly and wheeled it over to the reach-in cooler. When she opened the cooler, she noticed that it was tightly packed. However, she was able to squeeze the case into a spot on the top shelf.

Next, she wheeled several cases of fresh ground beef and the fresh salmon over to the walk-in cooler. She noticed that the readout on the outside of the cooler indicated 39°F (4°C). Alyce pushed through the cold curtains and bumped into a hot stockpot of soup as she moved inside. She moved the soup over and made a space for the ground beef. She was able to put the salmon on the shelf above the soup. Alyce said hello to Mary, who had just cleaned the shelving in the unit and was lining it with new aluminum foil.

① What receiving mistakes did Alyce make?

_____

_____

_____

_____

_____

_____

_____

_____

_____

② What storage mistakes were made at the operation?

_____

_____

_____

_____

_____

_____

_____

_____

_____

For answers, please turn to page 5.19.

Study Questions

Circle the best answer to each question.

① **What is the most important factor in choosing a food supplier?**

  A It has a HACCP program or other food safety system.

  B It has documented manufacturing and packing practices.

  C Its warehouse is close to the operation, reducing shipping time.

  D It has been inspected and complies with local, state, and federal laws.

② **What is the best method of checking the temperature of a delivery of fresh fish?**

  A Feel the fish, making sure that it is cold to the touch.

  B Insert a thermometer probe into the thickest part of the fish.

  C Place a time-temperature indicator on the surface of the fish.

  D Use an infrared thermometer to check the fish's temperature.

③ **What is the correct temperature for receiving cold TCS food?**

  A 32°F (0°C) or lower

  B 41°F (5°C) or lower

  C 45°F (7°C) or lower

  D 50°F (10°C) or lower

④ **Milk can be received at 45°F (7°C) under what condition?**

  A It is thrown out after 2 days.

  B It is cooled to 41°F (5°C) or lower in 4 hours.

  C It is immediately cooled to 41°F (5°C) or lower.

  D It is served or used in the operation within 2 hours.

⑤ **Frozen shrimp is rejected during receiving for having large ice crystals on the food and packaging. What is the problem that caused this?**

  A Cross-contact

  B Cross-contamination

  C Time-temperature abuse

  D Incorrect cleaning and sanitizing

⑥ **What is required when receiving fish that will be served raw or partially cooked?**

  A It must be alive when received.

  B It must be thawed in the microwave.

  C It must be used within 24 hours of receiving.

  D It must be correctly frozen before you receive it.

⑦ **What must be included on the label of TCS food that was prepped in-house?**

   A Date that the food was received

   B Name of each TCS ingredient included

   C Date that the food should be thrown out

   D List of all potential ingredients in the food

⑧ **How long can TCS food that was prepped in-house be stored?**

   A 3 days

   B 5 days

   C 7 days

   D 9 days

⑨ **When storing food using the FIFO method, where should the food with the earliest use-by dates be stored?**

   A Below food with later use-by dates

   B Behind food with later use-by dates

   C In front of food with later use-by dates

   D Alongside food with later use-by dates

⑩ **What is the problem with storing raw ground beef above prepped salads?**

   A Cross-contamination

   B Poor personal hygiene

   C Time-temperature abuse

   D Cross-contact with allergens

⑪ **In top-to-bottom order, how should a fresh pork roast, fresh salmon, a container of lettuce, and a pan of fresh chicken breasts be stored in a cooler?**

   A Lettuce, fresh salmon, fresh pork roast, fresh chicken breasts

   B Fresh salmon, fresh pork roast, fresh chicken breasts, lettuce

   C Lettuce, fresh chicken breasts, fresh pork roast, fresh salmon

   D Fresh salmon, lettuce, fresh chicken breasts, fresh pork roast

⑫ **How many inches (centimeters) from the floor should food be stored?**

   A At least 1" (3 cm)

   B At least 2" (5 cm)

   C At least 4" (10 cm)

   D At least 6" (15 cm)

For answers, please turn to page 5.19.

Answers

5.7   Accept or Reject?

① R   ⑥ R

② R   ⑦ R

③ A   ⑧ R

④ A   ⑨ R

⑤ R   ⑩ R

5.12   Load the Cooler

① C   ④ D

② E   ⑤ B

③ A

5.12   What's Wrong with This Picture?

Here are the unsafe storage practices.

- Chemicals stored with food
- Food stored on the floor
- Boxes of food not labeled
- Spilled food not cleaned up
- Cooler door open
- Overstocked cooler
- Area not clean
- Unlabeled items in cooler

5.14   Chapter Review Case Study

① Alyce made the following receiving mistakes.

- She should have rejected the shrimp. The ice crystals are evidence of thawing and re-freezing.

- She did not clean and sanitize the probe she had used to measure the temperature of the ground beef and the fish.

- She should have rejected the salmon. The temperature of the fish was above 41°F (5°C) and the melted ice could be evidence of time-temperature abuse.

- She felt the container of sour cream instead of measuring the internal temperature of the food.

- She should have rejected the torn carton of pasta.

- She put the cold food on the side while receiving the dry food.

② The operation made the following storage mistakes.

- The freezer door was left open.

- Alyce placed the case of sour cream into an already overloaded refrigerator.

- Alyce put the raw salmon above ready-to-eat food (soup).

- Alyce checked the cooler's readout temperature which was good, but she also should have spot-checked the internal temperatures of the food stored inside.

- A hot stockpot of soup was stored in the walk-in refrigerator. Hot food should never be placed in a refrigerator.

- Mary was lining the refrigerator shelving with aluminum foil. This can restrict airflow in the unit.

5.16   Study Questions

① D	④ B	⑦ C	⑩ A
② B	⑤ C	⑧ C	⑪ A
③ B	⑥ D	⑨ C	⑫ D

chapter 6
The Flow of Food: Preparation

Preparation	Cooking Food	Cooling and Reheating Food
— General Preparation Practices — Thawing — Prepping Specific Food — Preparation Practices That Have Special Requirements	— How to Check Temperatures — Cooking Requirements for Specific Food — Consumer Advisories — Operations That Mainly Serve High-Risk Populations	— Temperature Requirements for Cooling Food — Methods for Cooling Food — Reheating Food

((NEWS)) Undercooked Meatballs Result in Fatal Outbreak

A 73-year-old woman died and 51 people were hospitalized after eating undercooked turkey meatballs at a buffet in the southeastern United States. The victims all got sick with *Salmonella*. An investigation revealed that the chef had browned the meatballs but failed to finish baking them. This left the centers of the meatballs undercooked.

You Can Prevent This

The illness in the story above could have been avoided if the chef had made sure that the meatballs were cooked to the correct internal temperature. In this chapter, you will learn about the specific cooking temperatures that can keep food safe. You will also learn other guidelines for keeping food safe during preparation.

- Preventing cross-contamination and time-temperature abuse

- Thawing food correctly

- Cooking food to a minimum internal temperature

- Cooling and reheating food to the correct temperature in the correct amount of time

Preparation	Cooking Food	Cooling and Reheating Food
— General Preparation Practices — Thawing — Prepping Specific Food — Preparation Practices That Have Special Requirements	— How to Check Temperatures — Cooking Requirements for Specific Food — Consumer Advisories — Operations That Mainly Serve High-Risk Populations	— Temperature Requirements for Cooling Food — Methods for Cooling Food — Reheating Food

Preparation

Cross-contamination and time-temperature abuse can happen easily when you are preparing food. But, you can prevent pathogens from spreading and growing by making good food-prep choices.

General Preparation Practices

No matter what type of food you are prepping, you should begin by following these guidelines.

Equipment   Make sure workstations, cutting boards, and utensils are clean and sanitized.

Quantity   Only remove as much food from the cooler as you can prep in a short period of time. This keeps ingredients from sitting out for long periods of time. In the photo at left, the food handler has taken out too much tuna salad.

Storage   Return prepped food to the cooler, or cook it as quickly as possible.

Additives   If you use food or color additives when prepping food, follow these guidelines.

- Only use additives that have been approved by your local regulatory authority. NEVER use more than is allowed by law. NEVER use additives to alter the appearance of the food.

- Do NOT sell produce that was treated with sulfites before it was received in the operation. NEVER add sulfites to produce that will be eaten raw.

Presentation   Food must be offered to customers in a way that does not mislead or misinform them. Customers must be able to judge the true appearance, color, and quality of food. Do NOT use the following to misrepresent the appearance of food.

- Food additives or color additives

- Colored overwraps

- Lights

Food that has not been honestly presented must be thrown out.

Corrective actions   Food that has become unsafe must be thrown out unless it can be safely reconditioned. All food—especially ready-to-eat food—must be thrown out in the following situations.

- When it is handled by staff who have been restricted or excluded from the operation due to illness

- When it is contaminated by hands or bodily fluids from the nose or mouth

- When it has exceeded the time and temperature requirements designed to keep food safe

Sometimes food can be restored to a safe condition. This is called reconditioning. For example, a hot food that has not been held at the correct temperature may be reheated if it has not been in the temperature danger zone for more than two hours. This can return food to a safe condition.

Thawing

When frozen food is thawed and exposed to the temperature danger zone, pathogens in the food will begin to grow. To reduce this growth, NEVER thaw food at room temperature. Thaw TCS food in the following ways.

Refrigeration   Thaw food in a cooler, keeping its temperature at 41°F (5°C) or lower.

Running water   Submerge food under running, drinkable water at 70°F (21°C) or lower. The flow of the water must be strong enough to wash loose food bits into the drain. Always use a clean and sanitized food-prep sink when thawing food this way. NEVER let the temperature of the food go above 41°F (5°C) for longer than four hours.

This includes the time it takes to thaw the food plus the time it takes to prep or cool it. The photo at left shows the correct way to thaw food under running water.

Microwave   Thaw food in a microwave oven if it will be cooked immediately after thawing. The food must be cooked in conventional cooking equipment, such as an oven, once it's thawed.

Cooking   Thaw food as part of the cooking process.

Thawing ROP Fish

Frozen fish may be supplied in reduced-oxygen packaging (ROP). This fish should usually remain frozen until ready for use. If this is stated on the label, the fish must be removed from the packaging at the following times.

- Before thawing it under refrigeration

- Before or immediately after thawing it under running water

Prepping Specific Food

Special care must be taken when handling ice and when preparing produce, eggs, and salads that contain TCS food.

Produce

When prepping produce, follow these guidelines.

Cross-contamination   Make sure fruit and vegetables do **NOT** touch surfaces exposed to raw meat, seafood, or poultry.

Washing   Wash produce thoroughly under running water. This is especially important before cutting, cooking, or combining it with other ingredients.

- The water should be a little warmer than the produce.

- Pay special attention to leafy greens such as lettuce and spinach, as the food handler in the photo at left is doing. Remove the outer leaves, and pull the lettuce or spinach completely apart and rinse thoroughly.

- Certain chemicals may be used to wash fruits and vegetables. Also, produce can be treated by washing it in water containing ozone. This treatment helps control pathogens.

Check your local regulatory requirements.

Soaking or storing   When soaking or storing produce in standing water or an ice-water slurry, do **NOT** mix different items or multiple batches of the same item.

Fresh-cut produce   Refrigerate and hold sliced melons, cut tomatoes, and cut leafy greens at 41°F (5°C) or lower. Many operations hold other fresh-cut produce at this temperature as well.

Raw seed sprouts   If your operation primarily serves high-risk populations, do **NOT** serve raw seed sprouts.

Eggs and Egg Mixtures

When prepping eggs and egg mixtures, follow these guidelines.

Pooled eggs   Handle pooled eggs (if allowed by your local regulatory authority) carefully. Pooled eggs are eggs that are cracked open and combined in a container, as shown in the photo at left. Cook them promptly after mixing, or store them at 41°F (5°C) or lower. Clean and sanitize the containers used to hold them before making a new batch.

Pasteurized eggs   Consider using pasteurized shell eggs or egg products when prepping egg dishes that need little or no cooking. Examples include Caesar salad dressing, hollandaise sauce, tiramisu, and mousse.

High-risk populations   If you mainly serve high-risk populations, such as those in hospitals and nursing homes, use pasteurized eggs or egg products when serving dishes that are raw or undercooked. Shell eggs that are pooled must also be pasteurized. You may use unpasteurized shell eggs if the dish will be cooked all the way through, such as an omelet or a cake.

Salads Containing TCS Food

Chicken, tuna, egg, pasta, and potato salads have all been involved in foodborne-illness outbreaks. These salads are not usually cooked after preparation. This means you do not have a chance to reduce pathogens, such as *Staphylococcus aureus*, that may have gotten into the salad. Therefore, you must take a few extra steps. Follow these guidelines.

Using leftovers   TCS food such as pasta, chicken, and potatoes can be used only if it has been cooked, held, and cooled correctly.

Storing leftovers   Throw out leftover food held at 41°F (5°C) or lower after seven days. Check the use-by date before using stored food items.

Ice

Follow these guidelines to avoid contaminating ice in your operation.

Consumption   Make ice from water that is safe to drink.

Cooling food   **NEVER** use ice as an ingredient if it was used to keep food cold. For example, if ice is used to cool food on a salad bar, it cannot then be used in drinks.

Containers and scoops   Use clean and sanitized containers and ice scoops to transfer ice from an ice machine to other containers.

* Store ice scoops outside of the ice machine in a clean, protected location, as shown in the photo at left.

* **NEVER** hold or carry ice in containers that have held raw meat, seafood, or poultry; or chemicals.

* **NEVER** touch ice with hands or use a glass to scoop ice.

Preparation Practices That Have Special Requirements

You will need a variance when prepping food in certain ways. A variance is a document issued by your regulatory authority that allows a regulatory requirement to be waived or changed.

When applying for a variance, your regulatory authority may require you to submit a HACCP plan. The plan must account for any food safety risks related to the way you plan to prep the food item.

You will need a variance if your operation plans to prep food in any of the following ways.

- Packaging fresh juice on-site for sale at a later time, unless the juice has a warning label.

- Smoking food as a way to preserve it (but not to enhance flavor), as shown in the photo at left.

- Using food additives or adding components such as vinegar to preserve or alter the food so that it no longer needs time and temperature control for safety.

- Curing food.

- Custom-processing animals for personal use. For example, a hunter brings a deer to a restaurant for dressing and takes the meat home for later use.

- Packaging food using a reduced-oxygen packaging (ROP) method. This includes MAP, vacuum-packed, and *sous vide* food. *Clostridium botulinum* and *Listeria monocytogenes* are risks to food packaged in these ways.

- Sprouting seeds or beans.

- Offering live shellfish from a display tank.

Apply Your Knowledge

What's the Problem?

① Reggie filled a clean and sanitized sink with cold water and ice. Then he soaked a partial case of green onions that he had gotten from the cooler and a new case of onions delivered that morning together.

Was the food prepped correctly?_____

Why or why not?_____

_____

② Linda needed to make 20 box lunches to be picked up in 3 hours. She got out the bread, meat, and cheese, and left them on the prep table so that she could make the sandwiches in between her other tasks.

Was the food prepped correctly?_____

Why or why not?_____

_____

③ Brandon trimmed an uncooked roast on the red cutting board. Then he washed his hands and used a different knife to slice tomatoes on the green cutting board.

Was the food prepped correctly?_____

Why or why not?_____

_____

④ Jessica read an article about sprouting beans. It inspired her to try it in her operation. She used some of the freshly sprouted beans in one of her daily specials.

Was the food prepped correctly?_____

Why or why not?_____

_____

⑤ Norris wanted to make his famous Eggs Benedict for the residents at the nursing home where he works. He mixed egg yolks from raw shell eggs with butter and lemon juice and poured the uncooked sauce over several hotel pans of poached eggs.

Was the food prepped correctly?_____

Why or why not?_____

_____

For answers, please turn to page 6.24.

Apply Your Knowledge

Pick the Correct Way to Prep Food

Write an ✘ next to the correct answer in each pair.

① To thaw frozen food:

_____ Ⓐ   Place the item on a prep table at room temperature.

_____ Ⓑ   Place the item in a cooler which keeps it at 41°F (5°C) or lower.

② To preserve food by smoking it:

_____ Ⓐ   Make sure the item has been thawed before smoking it.

_____ Ⓑ   Make sure you contact your local regulatory authority to get a variance.

③ When using leftovers of TCS food to make salads:

_____ Ⓐ   Make sure to throw out leftovers held at 41°F (5°C) or lower after 7 days.

_____ Ⓑ   Make sure to throw out leftovers held at 41°F (5°C) or lower after 10 days.

④ When using pooled eggs:

_____ Ⓐ   Cook them promptly after mixing, or store them at room temperature.

_____ Ⓑ   Cook them promptly after mixing, or store them at 41°F (5°C) or lower.

Handling Ice

Write an ✘ next to each unsafe practice when handling ice.

① _____

② _____

③ _____

④ _____

For answers, please turn to page 6.24.

Preparation	Cooking Food	Cooling and Reheating Food
— General Preparation Practices — Thawing — Prepping Specific Food — Preparation Practices That Have Special Requirements	— How to Check Temperatures — Cooking Requirements for Specific Food — Consumer Advisories — Operations That Mainly Serve High-Risk Populations	— Temperature Requirements for Cooling Food — Methods for Cooling Food — Reheating Food

Cooking Food

The only way to reduce pathogens in food to safe levels is to cook it to its minimum internal temperature. This temperature is different for each food. Once reached, you must hold the food at this temperature for a specific amount of time. If customers request a lower temperature, you need to inform them of the potential risk of foodborne illness. Also be aware of special menu restrictions if you serve high-risk populations.

While cooking reduces pathogens in food, it does not destroy spores or toxins they may have produced. You still must handle food correctly before you cook it.

How to Check Temperatures

To make sure the food you are cooking has reached the correct temperature, you must know how to take the temperature correctly. Follow these guidelines.

Pick a thermometer with a probe that is the correct size for the food.

Check the temperature in the thickest part of the food.

Take at least two readings in different locations.

Cooking Requirements for Specific Food

Monitor the temperature of cooked food to make sure it has reached the correct temperature. Minimum temperatures have been developed for TCS food. These temperatures are listed on the next page. However, your operation or area might require different temperatures.

Check your local regulatory requirements.

Cooking Requirements for Specific Types of Food

Minimum Internal Temperature	Type of Food
165°F (74°C) for 15 seconds	• Poultry—including whole or ground chicken, turkey, or duck • Stuffing made with fish, meat, or poultry • Stuffed meat, seafood, poultry, or pasta • Dishes that include previously cooked TCS ingredients (raw ingredients should be cooked to their minimum internal temperatures)
155°F (68°C) for 15 seconds	• Ground meat—including beef, pork, and other meat • Injected meat—including brined ham and flavor-injected roasts • Mechanically tenderized meat • Ratites—including ostrich and emu • Ground seafood—including chopped or minced seafood • Shell eggs that will be hot-held for service
145°F (63°C) for 15 seconds	• Seafood—including fish, shellfish, and crustaceans • Steaks/chops of pork, beef, veal, and lamb • Commercially raised game • Shell eggs that will be served immediately
145°F (63°C) for 4 minutes	• Roasts of pork, beef, veal, and lamb • Roasts may be cooked to these alternate cooking times and temperatures depending on the type of roast and oven used: 130°F (54°C) 112 minutes 131°F (55°C) 89 minutes 133°F (56°C) 56 minutes 135°F (57°C) 36 minutes 136°F (58°C) 28 minutes 138°F (59°C) 18 minutes 140°F (60°C) 12 minutes 142°F (61°C) 8 minutes 144°F (62°C) 5 minutes
135°F (57°C)	• Fruit, vegetables, grains (rice, pasta), and legumes (beans, refried beans) that will be hot-held for service

Cooking TCS Food in the Microwave Oven

Meat, seafood, poultry, and eggs that you cook in a microwave oven must be cooked to 165°F (74°C). In addition, follow these guidelines.

- Cover the food to prevent its surface from drying out.

- Rotate or stir it halfway through the cooking process so that the heat reaches the food more evenly.

- Let the covered food stand for at least two minutes after cooking to let the food temperature even out.

- Check the temperature in at least two places to make sure that the food is cooked through.

Partial Cooking During Preparation

Some operations partially cook food during prep and then finish cooking it just before service. You must follow the steps below if you plan to partially cook meat, seafood, poultry, or eggs; or dishes containing these items.

1 Do not cook the food for longer than 60 minutes during initial cooking.

2 Cool the food immediately after initial cooking.

3 Freeze or refrigerate the food after cooling it. If refrigerating the food, make sure it is held at 41°F (5°C) or lower.

4 Heat the food to its required minimum internal temperature before selling or serving it.

5 Cool the food if it will not be served immediately or held for service.

Your local regulatory authority may require you to have written procedures that explain how the food cooked by this process will be prepped and stored. These procedures must be approved by the regulatory authority and describe the following.

- How the requirements will be monitored and documented
- Which corrective actions will be taken if requirements are not met
- How these food items will be marked after initial cooking to indicate that they need further cooking
- How these food items will be separated from ready-to-eat food during storage, once initial cooking is complete

Consumer Advisories

You must cook TCS food to the minimum internal temperatures listed in this chapter unless a customer requests otherwise. This might happen often in your operation, particularly if you serve meat, eggs, or seafood.

Disclosure   If your menu includes TCS items that are raw or undercooked, you must note it on the menu next to these items. This can be done by placing an asterisk next to the item that points customers to a footnote at the bottom of the menu. The footnote must include a statement that indicates the item is raw or undercooked, or contains raw or undercooked ingredients. The menu in the photo at left shows an example of disclosure.

Reminder   You must advise customers who order food that is raw or undercooked of the increased risk of foodborne illness. You can do this by posting a notice in your menu. You can also provide this information using brochures, table tents, signs, or other written methods.

Check your local regulatory requirements.

Children's Menus

The Food and Drug Administration (FDA) advises against offering raw or undercooked meat, poultry, seafood, or eggs on a children's menu. This is especially true for undercooked ground beef, which may be contaminated with shiga toxin-producing *E. coli* O157:H7.

Operations That Mainly Serve High-Risk Populations

Operations that mainly serve a high-risk population, such as nursing homes or day-care centers, cannot serve certain items. NEVER serve raw seed sprouts or raw or undercooked eggs, meat, or seafood. Examples include over-easy eggs, raw oysters on the half shell, and rare hamburgers.

Apply Your Knowledge

How Do You Check It?

Identify the pictures that show the correct way to check a temperature. Write your answers in the blanks provided.

① _____

Ⓐ

Ⓑ

② _____

Ⓐ

Ⓑ

For answers, please turn to page 6.24.

Apply Your Knowledge

What's the Temperature?

Identify the minimum internal cooking temperature for each food. Write the letter in the space provided. Some letters will be used more than once.

Ⓐ 135°F (57°C)

Ⓑ 145°F (63°C)

Ⓒ 155°F (68°C)

Ⓓ 165°F (74°C)

① _____ Salmon steak

② _____ Roasted vegetables that will be hot-held

③ _____ Ground pork

④ _____ Lamb chops

⑤ _____ Eggs for immediate service

⑥ _____ Duck

⑦ _____ Pasta

⑧ _____ Beef steak

⑨ _____ Chicken enchiladas made with previously cooked chicken

⑩ _____ Pork loin injected with marinade

⑪ _____ Broccoli cooked in a microwave oven that will be hot-held

⑫ _____ Ostrich filet

⑬ _____ Wild rice that will be hot-held

⑭ _____ Ravioli stuffed with cheese

⑮ _____ Buffalo steak (commercially raised buffalo)

For answers, please turn to page 6.24.

Preparation	Cooking Food	Cooling and Reheating Food
— General Preparation Practices — Thawing — Prepping Specific Food — Preparation Practices That Have Special Requirements	— How to Check Temperatures — Cooking Requirements for Specific Food — Consumer Advisories — Operations That Mainly Serve High-Risk Populations	— Temperature Requirements for Cooling Food — Methods for Cooling Food — Reheating Food

Cooling and Reheating Food

When you don't serve cooked food immediately, you must get it out of the temperature danger zone as quickly as possible. That means cooling it quickly. You also need to reheat it correctly, especially if you are going to hold it.

Temperature Requirements for Cooling Food

As you know, pathogens grow well in the temperature danger zone. However, they grow much faster at temperatures between 125°F and 70°F (52°C and 21°C). Food must pass through this temperature range quickly to reduce this growth.

Cool TCS food from 135°F (57°C) to 41°F (5°C) or lower within six hours.

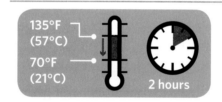

First, cool food from 135°F to 70°F (57°C to 21°C) within two hours.

Then cool it from 70°F to 41°F (21°C to 5°C) or lower in the next four hours.

If food has not reached 70°F (21°C) within two hours, it must be reheated and then cooled again.

If you can cool the food from 135°F to 70°F (57°C to 21°C) in less than two hours, you can use the remaining time to cool it to 41°F (5°C) or lower. However, the total cooling time cannot be longer than six hours. For example, if you cool food from 135°F to 70°F (57°C to 21°C) in one hour, you have the remaining five hours to get the food to 41°F (5°C) or lower.

Check your local regulatory requirements.

Methods for Cooling Food

The following factors affect how quickly food will cool.

Thickness or density of the food   The denser the food, the more slowly it will cool.

Size of the food   Large food items cool more slowly than smaller items. To let food cool faster, you should reduce its size. Cut large food items into smaller pieces. Divide large containers of food into smaller containers or shallow pans, as shown in the photo at left.

Storage container   Stainless steel transfers heat away from food faster than plastic. Shallow pans let the heat from food disperse faster than deep pans.

NEVER cool large amounts of hot food in a cooler. Most coolers are not designed to cool large amounts of hot food quickly. Also, placing hot food in a cooler may not move the food through the temperature danger zone quickly enough. Here are some effective methods for cooling food quickly and safely.

Ice-water bath   After dividing food into smaller containers, place them in a clean prep sink or large pot filled with ice water. The food handler in the photo at left is cooling a container of meat sauce this way.

Stir the food frequently to cool it faster and more evenly.

Blast chiller   Blast chillers blast cold air across food at high speeds to remove heat. They are typically used to cool large amounts of food.

Ice paddle   Plastic paddles are available that can be filled with ice or with water and then frozen. Food stirred with these paddles will cool quickly, as shown in the photo at left.

Food cools even faster when placed in an ice-water bath and stirred with an ice paddle.

Ice or cold water as ingredient   When cooling soups or stews, the recipe is made with less water than required. Cold water or ice is then added after cooking to cool the food and provide the remaining water.

Storing Food for Further Cooling

Loosely cover food containers before storing them. Food can be left uncovered if stored in a way that prevents contaminants from getting into it. Storing uncovered containers above other food, especially raw seafood, meat, and poultry, will help prevent cross-contamination.

Reheating Food

How you reheat food depends on how you intend to use the food. Follow these guidelines when reheating food.

Food reheated for immediate service   You can reheat food that will be served immediately, such as beef for a beef sandwich, to any temperature. However, you must make sure the food was cooked and cooled correctly.

Food reheated for hot-holding   You must heat TCS food for hot-holding to an internal temperature of 165°F (74°C) for 15 seconds. Make sure the food reaches this temperature within two hours from start to finish. The food handler in the photo at left is reheating clam chowder for hot-holding. These guidelines apply to all reheating methods, such as ovens or microwave ovens.

Reheat commercially processed and packaged ready-to-eat food to an internal temperature of at least 135°F (57°C). This includes items such as cheese sticks and deep-fried vegetables.

Apply Your Knowledge

Cooling Food

Write an ✘ next to each food that has been cooled correctly.

 ① _____

Meat sauce was cooled from 135°F to 70°F (57°C to 21°C) in 1 hour and then from 70°F to 41°F (21°C to 5°C) in 4 hours.

 ② _____

Chili was cooled from 135°F to 70°F (57°C to 21°C) in 2 hours and then from 70°F to 41°F (21°C to 5°C) in 4 hours.

For answers, please turn to page 6.24.

Apply Your Knowledge

Is It Hot Enough?

Decide if the food in each situation is safe to serve. Explain why or why not.

① At 9:00 a.m., Lin clocked in, said hello to her manager, and started to set up the buffet. Fifteen minutes later, she headed to the walk-in cooler, where she grabbed a stockpot of chili that had been made a few days earlier. She placed the stockpot on the stove and started reheating it. At 11:30 a.m., she checked the temperature of the chili, which had reached 155°F (68°C). Satisfied, she moved on to her next task.

Is the chili safe to serve? _____

Why or why not? _____

_____

_____

② Thursday at lunch, a customer ordered a stacked hot roast beef and cheddar sandwich. Mina took precooked slices of beef from the reach-in cooler and put them in a bain of hot au jus. She heated the slices of beef for a few minutes. Then she made the sandwich, topping it with melted cheddar, and placed it on the counter for pickup.

Is the sandwich safe to serve? _____

Why or why not? _____

_____

_____

_____

For answers, please turn to page 6.24.

Chapter Summary

- To protect food during preparation, you must handle it safely. The keys are time and temperature control and preventing cross-contamination.

- Freezing does not kill pathogens. Pathogens in the food will grow if exposed to the temperature danger zone during thawing. Thaw frozen food in the cooler, under running water, in a microwave oven, or as part of the cooking process. Never thaw food at room temperature.

- Prevent cross-contamination and time-temperature abuse when preparing food. Prep food in small batches and keep workstations and utensils clean and sanitized. Prepped food that is not going to be cooked immediately should be put back in the cooler.

- Cooking food can reduce pathogens in food to safe levels. You must cook food to minimum internal temperatures for a specific amount of time. These temperatures vary from food to food. Cooking does not kill the spores or toxins that some pathogens produce.

- You must advise customers who order food that is raw or undercooked of the increased risk of foodborne illness. You can do this in different ways. If your menu includes TCS items that are raw or undercooked, you must note it on the menu next to these items. The FDA advises against offering raw and undercooked food on children's menus.

- TCS food must be cooled from 135°F to 70°F (57°C to 21°C) within two hours. Then it must be cooled from 70°F to 41°F (21°C to 5°C) or lower in the next four hours.

- Before food is cooled, you should reduce its size. Cut large food items into smaller pieces. Divide large containers of food into smaller ones. Use an ice-water bath, stir food with ice paddles, or use a blast or tumble chiller to cool food safely.

- Reheated TCS food that will be hot-held must be heated to an internal temperature of 165°F (74°C) for 15 seconds. Make sure the food reaches this temperature within two hours.

Chapter Review Case Study

You can avoid foodborne-illness outbreaks in your operation if you prepare food safely. Doing this includes following general practices for thawing and prepping food; cooking food thoroughly; and cooling and reheating food correctly.

Now, take what you have learned in this chapter and apply it to the following case study.

Angie had a busy day ahead of her at the Sunnydale Nursing Home. Looking in the freezer, Angie realized that she had forgotten to thaw the chicken breasts she planned to serve for dinner. Moving quickly, she placed the frozen chicken in a prep sink and turned on the hot water. While waiting for chicken to thaw, she grabbed a pan of leftover soup from the cooler and placed it in the steam table to heat up.

By 7:30 p.m., all the residents had eaten dinner. As Angie began cleaning up, she realized she had a lot of cooked chicken breasts leftover. Betty, the new assistant manager, had forgotten to tell Angie that several residents were going to a local festival and would miss dinner. "No problem," Angie thought. "We can use the leftover chicken to make chicken salad."

Angie left the still-hot chicken breasts in a pan on the prep table while she started putting other food away and cleaning up. At 9:45 p.m., when everything else was clean, she put her hand over the pan of chicken breasts and decided they were cool enough to handle. She covered the pan with plastic wrap and put it in the cooler.

Three days later, Angie came in to work the breakfast shift. As she started her shift, she decided to make chicken salad from the leftover chicken breasts. Angie took all the ingredients she needed for the chicken salad out of the cooler and put them on a prep table. Then she turned her attention to getting breakfast started.

First, she cracked three-dozen eggs into a large bowl, added some milk, and set the bowl near the stove. Then she took bacon out of the cooler and put it on the prep table next to the chicken-salad ingredients. She peeled off strips of bacon onto a sheet pan and put the pan into the oven. Then she went back to the stove to whisk the eggs and pour them onto the griddle. When they looked ready, Angie checked the temperature. The eggs had reached 145°F (63°C). Angie scooped the scrambled eggs into a hotel pan and put it in the steam table.

① What did Angie do wrong?

_____

_____

② What should Angie have done differently?

_____

_____

For answers, please turn to page 6.25.

Study Questions

Circle the best answer to each question.

① **What is the maximum water temperature allowed when thawing food under running water?**

  A 70°F (21°C)

  B 65°F (18°C)

  C 60°F (16°C)

  D 55°F (13°C)

② **What must food handlers do to food immediately after thawing it in the microwave oven?**

  A Hold it.

  B Cook it.

  C Cool it.

  D Freeze it.

③ **What can occur if prep tables are not cleaned and sanitized between uses?**

  A Off flavors in food

  B Cross-contamination

  C Toxic-metal poisoning

  D Time-temperature abuse

④ **A food handler thaws several frozen turkeys on a prep table. What is the danger that this poses to the food?**

  A Off flavors in food

  B Cross-contamination

  C Toxic-metal poisoning

  D Time-temperature abuse

⑤ **A food handler pulled a hotel pan of tuna salad from the cooler and used it to prepare six tuna salad sandwiches. What is the problem with this situation?**

  A Cross-contamination

  B Poor personal hygiene

  C Time-temperature abuse

  D Poor cleaning and sanitizing

⑥ **What is the minimum internal cooking temperature for stuffed pork chops?**

  A 135°F (57°C) for 15 seconds

  B 145°F (63°C) for 15 seconds

  C 155°F (68°C) for 15 seconds

  D 165°F (74°C) for 15 seconds

Continued on the next page ▶

► *Continued from previous page*

⑦ **What is the minimum internal cooking temperature for eggs, meat, poultry, and seafood cooked in a microwave oven?**

A 135°F (57°C)

B 145°F (63°C)

C 155°F (68°C)

D 165°F (74°C)

⑧ **What is the minimum internal cooking temperature for eggs that will be hot-held for service?**

A 135°F (57°C) for 15 seconds

B 145°F (63°C) for 15 seconds

C 155°F (68°C) for 15 seconds

D 165°F (74°C) for 15 seconds

⑨ **What is the minimum internal cooking temperature for ground beef?**

A 135°F (57°C) for 15 seconds

B 145°F (63°C) for 15 seconds

C 155°F (68°C) for 15 seconds

D 165°F (74°C) for 15 seconds

⑩ **Which food should not be offered on a children's menu: a rare hamburger, fried chicken tenders, grilled cheese sandwich, or spaghetti with meat sauce?**

A Rare hamburger

B Fried chicken tenders

C Grilled cheese sandwich

D Spaghetti with meat sauce

⑪ **A food handler can cool a stockpot of clam chowder by placing it into a**

A cooler.

B freezer.

C sink of ice water.

D cold-holding unit.

⑫ **What temperature must TCS food be reheated to if it will be hot-held?**

A 135°F (57°C) for 15 seconds

B 145°F (63°C) for 15 seconds

C 155°F (68°C) for 15 seconds

D 165°F (74°C) for 15 seconds

⑬ **A food handler is reheating commercially processed cheese sticks, which will be hot-held on a buffet. What temperature must the cheese sticks be reheated to?**

A   135°F (57°C)

B   145°F (63°C)

C   155°F (68°C)

D   165°F (74°C)

⑭ **When partially cooking food for later service, what is the maximum amount of time that the food can be heated during the initial cooking step?**

A   60 minutes

B   70 minutes

C   80 minutes

D   90 minutes

For answers, please turn to page 6.25.

Answers

6.7   What's the Problem?

① No. One batch of green onions could cross-contaminate the other. Between batches, he should have emptied the sink, cleaned and sanitized it, and changed the ice water.

② No. The meat and cheese are being time-temperature abused. She should take out of the cooler only what she can use within a short amount of time.

③ Yes. He used separate equipment for the meat and the produce.

④ No. She should have contacted her local regulatory authority before sprouting the beans. She would have needed a variance to do this.

⑤ No. Because he serves food at a nursing home, he cannot use raw shell eggs in dishes that will be served raw or undercooked. Also, poached shell eggs are undercooked and should not be served in a nursing home unless the eggs have been pasteurized.

6.8   Pick the Correct Way to Prep Food

① B		③ A	
② B		④ B	

6.8   Handling Ice

1, 2, and 4 should be marked.

6.13   How Do You Check It?

① A

② A

6.14   What's the Temperature?

① B	⑤ B	⑨ D	⑬ A
② A	⑥ D	⑩ C	⑭ D
③ C	⑦ A	⑪ A	⑮ B
④ B	⑧ B	⑫ C	

6.17   Cooling Food

1 and 2 should be marked.

6.18   Is It Hot Enough?

① No. The chili did not reach an internal temperature of 165°F (74°C) within two hours.

② Yes. Assuming the roast beef was cooked and cooled correctly, it can be reheated to any temperature because it is being served immediately.

6.20　Chapter Review Case Study

① Here is what Angie did wrong.

- She thawed the chicken breasts the wrong way. She should not have thawed them under hot water.

- She cooled the leftover chicken breasts the wrong way. She should not have left them out to cool at room temperature.

- She subjected the chicken salad ingredients to time-temperature abuse when she left them on the prep table.

- She pooled shell eggs when prepping the scrambled eggs. If shell eggs are going to be pooled when serving a high-risk population, such as the residents of a nursing home, they must be pasteurized. This became a bigger problem when Angie undercooked the eggs.

- She did not handle the pooled eggs correctly. She left the bowl in the temperature danger zone by putting it near a warm stove.

- She did not cook the scrambled eggs to the correct temperature before storing them on the steam table.

- She did not clean and sanitize the prep table after she made the bacon and before she chopped the celery and chicken.

② Here is what Angie should have done differently.

- If Angie needed to thaw the chicken breasts quickly, she should have either used a microwave or placed them under running water at 70°F (21°C) or lower.

- To cool the chicken breasts quickly for two-stage cooling, she could have used a blast chiller or placed the container of chicken breasts in an ice-water bath. Then she could move them to the cooler.

- She should have left the chicken salad ingredients in the cooler until she was ready to prep the salad.

- She should have used pasteurized shell eggs or egg products.

- She should have held the eggs in the cooler until she was ready to cook them.

- She should have cooked the eggs to be held for later service to at least 155°F (68°C) for 15 seconds.

- She should have cleaned and sanitized the prep table after she made the bacon and before she chopped the celery and chicken.

6.21　Study Questions

① A	⑤ C	⑨ C	⑬ A
② B	⑥ D	⑩ A	⑭ A
③ B	⑦ D	⑪ C	
④ D	⑧ C	⑫ D	

chapter 7
The Flow of Food: Service

Holding Food	Serving Food
— Guidelines for Holding Food	— Kitchen Staff Guidelines
— Holding Food Without	— Service Staff Guidelines
Temperature Control	— Self-Service Areas
	— Off-Site Service
	— Vending Machines

(((NEWS))) One Hundred Sickened by Norovirus Outbreak

A buffet attendant sickened over 100 guests at a large southwestern golf resort. Those that got sick had symptoms that included severe vomiting, diarrhea, and physical weakness. A food handler later tested positive for Norovirus. While the food handler was not experiencing symptoms at the time of the outbreak, he indicated that he had vomiting and diarrhea the week before.

Local regulatory authorities determined that the food handler contaminated items on the buffet line as he worked. The food handler failed to wash his hands correctly and change gloves as he moved from buffet station to buffet station. Authorities believed that utensils used by the guests had become contaminated by the food handler. This led to the outbreak.

You Can Prevent This

The operation in the story above had two problems. First, the food handler should have reported his illness the week before the outbreak. Second, the food handler should have been washing his hands and changing his gloves correctly while serving food.

Serving food the correct way would have helped prevent this outbreak. In this chapter, you will learn guidelines for keeping food safe after you have prepped and cooked it. These guidelines include the following.

- Holding hot food

- Holding cold food

- Using time as a method of control for food

- Preventing contamination of food in self-service areas and when serving food to customers

Holding Food	Serving Food
— Guidelines for Holding Food	— Kitchen Staff Guidelines
— Holding Food Without Temperature Control	— Service Staff Guidelines
	— Self-Service Areas
	— Off-Site Service
	— Vending Machines

Holding Food

Food that is being held for service is at risk for time-temperature abuse and cross-contamination. If your operation holds food, you must make policies that reduce these risks. Focus on time and temperature control, but don't forget about protecting the food from contamination. In some cases, you might be able to hold food without controlling its temperature.

Guidelines for Holding Food

Create policies about how long the operation will hold food. Also, create policies about when to throw away held food. For example, your policy may let you refill a pan of veal in a buffet all day, as long as you throw it out at the end of the day. Policies should also consider the following.

Food covers and sneeze guards   Cover food and install sneeze guards to protect food from contaminants. Covers, like the ones shown in the photo at left, also help maintain a food's internal temperature.

Temperature   Hold TCS food at the correct internal temperature.

- Hold hot food at 135°F (57°C) or higher. This will prevent pathogens such as *Bacillus cereus* from growing to unsafe levels.

- Hold cold food at 41°F (5°C) or lower. This will prevent pathogens such as *Staphylococcus aureus* from growing to unsafe levels.

Thermometer   Use a thermometer to check a food's internal temperature, as the food handler in the photo at left is doing. NEVER use the temperature gauge on a holding unit to do it. The gauge does not check the internal temperature of the food.

Time   Check food temperature at least every four hours.

- Throw out food that is not 41°F (5°C) or lower, or 135°F (57°C) or higher.

- You can also check the temperature every two hours. This will leave time for corrective action. For example, hot TCS food that has been held below 135°F (57°C) can be reheated and then placed back in the hot-holding unit.

Hot-holding equipment   NEVER use hot-holding equipment to reheat food unless it is built to do so. Most hot-holding equipment does not pass food through the temperature danger zone quickly enough. Reheat food correctly. Then move it to the holding unit.

Check your local regulatory requirements.

How This Relates to Me

At what temperature must your operation hold hot TCS food?

_____

At what temperature must your operation hold cold TCS food?

_____

Holding Food without Temperature Control

Your operation may want to display or hold TCS food without temperature control. Here are some examples of when you might hold food without temperature control.

- When displaying food for a short time, such as at an off-site catered event, as shown in the photo at left
- When electricity is not available to power holding equipment

If your operation displays or holds TCS food without temperature control, it must do so under certain conditions. Also note that the conditions for holding cold food are different from those for holding hot food.

Before using time as a method of control, check with your local regulatory authority for specific requirements.

Cold Food

You can hold cold food without temperature control for up to six hours if you meet these conditions.

- Hold the food at 41°F (5°C) or lower before removing it from refrigeration.
- Label the food with the time you removed it from refrigeration and the time you must throw it out. The discard time on the label must be six hours from the time you removed the food from refrigeration, as shown in the photo at left. For example, if you remove potato salad from refrigeration at 3:00 p.m. to serve at a picnic, the discard time on the label should be 9:00 p.m. This equals six hours from the time you removed it from refrigeration.
- Make sure the food temperature does not exceed 70°F (21°C) while it is being served. Throw out any food that exceeds this temperature.
- Sell, serve, or throw out the food within six hours.

Hot Food

You can hold hot food without temperature control for up to four hours if you meet these conditions.

- Hold the food at 135°F (57°C) or higher before removing it from temperature control.

- Label the food with the time you must throw it out. The discard time on the label must be four hours from the time you removed the food from temperature control, as shown in the photo at left.

- Sell, serve, or throw out the food within four hours.

How This Relates to Me

Does your jurisdiction allow you to hold ready-to-eat TCS food without temperature control?

_____

If yes, what are the requirements for doing so?

_____

_____

_____

Apply Your Knowledge

Is It Being Handled Safely?

Write an ✖ next to each food item that is not being handled safely.

① _____   Soup held at 120°F (49°C)

③ _____   Potato salad held at 75°F (24°C)

② _____   Pasta salad held at 39°F (4°C)

④ _____   Soup placed in a hot-holding unit at 40°F (4°C)

For answers, please turn to page 7.15.

Holding Food	Serving Food
— Guidelines for Holding Food	— Kitchen Staff Guidelines
— Holding Food Without Temperature Control	— Service Staff Guidelines
	— Self-Service Areas
	— Off-Site Service
	— Vending Machines

Serving Food

The biggest threat to food that is ready to be served is contamination. Your kitchen and service staff must know how to serve food in ways that keep it safe. Dining rooms, self-service areas, off-site locations, and vending machines all have specific guidelines that staff must follow.

Kitchen Staff Guidelines

Train your kitchen staff to serve food in these ways.

Bare-hand contact with food   Food handlers must wear single-use gloves whenever handling ready-to-eat food. As an alternative, food can be handled with spatulas, tongs, deli sheets, or other utensils. The photo at left shows two ways to avoid bare-hand contact. Keep in mind that there are some situations where it may be acceptable to handle ready-to-eat food with bare hands. For example, when a dish does not contain raw meat, seafood, or poultry, but will be cooked to at least 145°F (63°C).

Check your local regulatory requirements.

Clean and sanitized utensils   Use separate utensils for each food item. Clean and sanitize them after each serving task. If using utensils continuously, clean and sanitize them at least once every four hours.

Serving utensils   Store serving utensils in the food with the handle extended above the rim of the container, as shown in the photo at left. You can also place them on a clean and sanitized food-contact surface. Spoons or scoops used to serve food such as ice cream or mashed potatoes can be stored under running water. They can also be stored in a container of water that is maintained at a temperature of at least 135°C (57°C).

Refilling take-home containers   Some jurisdictions allow food handlers to refill take-home containers brought back by a customer with food and beverages. Take-home containers can be refilled if they meet these conditions.

* They were designed to be reused
* They were provided to the customer by the operation
* They are cleaned and sanitized correctly

Take-home beverage containers can also be refilled as long as the beverage is not a TCS food and the container will be refilled for the same customer. The container must also meet these conditions.

* It can be effectively cleaned at home and in the operation
* It will be rinsed before refilling with fresh, hot water under pressure
* It will be refilled by staff in the operation or by the customer using a process that prevents contamination

Service Staff Guidelines

Service staff must be as careful as kitchen staff. They can contaminate food simply by handling the food-contact areas of glasses, dishes, and utensils. Service staff should use these guidelines when serving food.

Hold dishes by the bottom or edge.

Hold glasses by the middle, bottom, or stem.

Do **NOT** touch the food-contact areas of dishes or glassware.

Carry glasses in a rack or on a tray to avoid touching the food-contact surfaces.

Do **NOT** stack glasses when carrying them.

Hold flatware by the handle.

Do **NOT** hold flatware by food-contact surfaces.

Store flatware so that servers grasp handles, not food-contact surfaces.

Avoid bare-hand contact with food that is ready to eat.

Use ice scoops or tongs to get ice.

NEVER scoop ice with your bare hands or a glass. A glass may chip or break.

Preset Tableware

If your operation presets tableware on dining tables, you must take steps to prevent it from becoming contaminated. This might include wrapping or covering the items as shown in the photo at left.

Table settings do not need to be wrapped or covered if extra, or unused, settings meet these requirements.

- They are removed when guests are seated.
- If they remain on the table, they are cleaned and sanitized after guests have left.

Re-serving Food

Service and kitchen staff should also know the rules about re-serving food previously served to another customer.

Menu items   Do **NOT** re-serve food returned by one customer to another customer.

Condiments   You must protect condiments from contamination. Serve them in their original containers or in containers designed to prevent contamination. Offering condiments in individual packets or portions can also help keep them safe. **NEVER** re-serve uncovered condiments. Do **NOT** combine leftover condiments with fresh ones, like the food handler in the photo at left is doing. Throw away opened portions or dishes of condiments after serving them to customers. Salsa, butter, mayonnaise, and ketchup are examples.

Bread or rolls   Do **NOT** re-serve uneaten bread to other customers. Change linens used in bread baskets after each customer.

Garnishes   **NEVER** re-serve plate garnishes, such as fruit or pickles, to another customer. Throw out served but unused garnishes.

Prepackaged food   In general, you may re-serve only unopened, prepackaged food in good condition. These include condiment packets and wrapped crackers. You may re-serve bottles of ketchup, mustard, and other condiments. The containers must remain closed between uses.

Self-Service Areas

Self-service areas can be contaminated easily. Follow these guidelines to prevent contamination and time-temperature abuse.

Protection   Food on display can be protected from contamination using sneeze guards. They should be located 14 inches (36 centimeters) above the counter and should extend 7 inches (18 centimeters) beyond the food, as shown in the photo at left. Food can also be protected by placing it in display cases or by packaging it in a way that will protect it from contamination. Whole, raw fruits and vegetables and nuts in the shell that require peeling or hulling before eating do not require the protection measures discussed above.

Labels   Label food located in self-service areas. For example, place the name of the food, such as types of salad dressing, on ladle handles.

Temperature   Keep hot food hot, 135°F (57°C) or higher. Keep cold food cold, 41°F (5°C) or lower.

Raw and ready-to-eat food   Typically, raw, unpackaged meat, poultry, and seafood cannot be offered for self-service. However, these items are an exception.

- Ready-to-eat food at buffets or salad bars that serve food such as sushi or raw shellfish

- Ready-to-cook portions that will be cooked and eaten immediately on the premises, such as at Mongolian barbeques

- Raw, frozen, shell-on shrimp or lobster

Refills   Do **NOT** let customers refill dirty plates or use dirty utensils at self-service areas. Pathogens such as Norovirus can easily be transferred by reused plates and utensils. Assign a staff member to monitor guests. Post signs reminding customers not to reuse plates and utensils.

Utensils   Stock food displays with the correct utensils for dispensing food. This might include tongs, ladles, or deli sheets.

Ice   Ice used to keep food or beverages cold should **NEVER** be used as an ingredient.

Labeling Bulk Food

Bulk food in self-service areas must be labeled. The label must be in plain view of the customer. When labeling food, you can include the manufacturer or processor label provided with the food. As an alternative, you can provide this information using a card, sign, or other labeling method.

Bulk unpackaged food, such as bakery products and unpackaged food portioned for customers, does not need to be labeled if it meets these conditions.

* The product makes no claim regarding health or nutrient content.
* There are no laws requiring labeling.
* The food is manufactured or prepared on the premises.
* The food is manufactured or prepared at another food operation or processing plant owned by the same person. The operation must be regulated.

Off-Site Service

Delays from the point of preparation to the point of service increase the risk that food will be exposed to contamination or time-temperature abuse. To transport correctly, follow these procedures.

Food containers   Pack food in insulated food containers. Use only food-grade containers, such as those shown in the photo at left. They should be designed so food cannot mix, leak, or spill. At the service site, use appropriate containers or equipment to hold food at the correct temperature.

Delivery vehicles   Clean the inside of delivery vehicles regularly.

Internal temperature   Check internal food temperatures. If containers or delivery vehicles are not holding food at the correct temperature, reevaluate the length of the delivery route or the efficiency of the equipment being used.

Labels   Label food with a use-by date and time, and reheating and service instructions for staff at off-site locations. This is shown in the photo at left.

Utilities   Make sure the service site has the correct utilities.

* Safe water for cooking, dishwashing, and handwashing
* Garbage containers stored away from food-prep, storage, and serving areas

Storage   Store raw meat, poultry, and seafood and ready-to-eat items separately. For example, store raw chicken separately from ready-to-eat salads.

Vending Machines

Handle food prepped and packaged for vending machines with the same care as any other food served to customers. Vending operators should protect food from contamination and time-temperature abuse during transport, delivery, and service. To keep vended food safe, follow these guidelines.

- Check product shelf life daily. Products often have a code date, such as an expiration or use-by date, like that shown in the photo at left. If the date has expired, throw out the food immediately. Throw out refrigerated food prepped on-site if not sold within seven days of preparation.

- Keep TCS food at the correct temperature. It should be held at 41°F (5°C) or lower, or at 135°F (57°C) or higher. These machines must have controls that prevent TCS food from being dispensed if the temperature stays in the danger zone for a specified amount of time. This food must be thrown out.

- Dispense TCS food in its original container.

- Wash and wrap fresh fruit with edible peels before putting it in a machine.

Apply Your Knowledge

Is It Being Served Safely?

Write an ✗ next to each food item that is not being served safely.

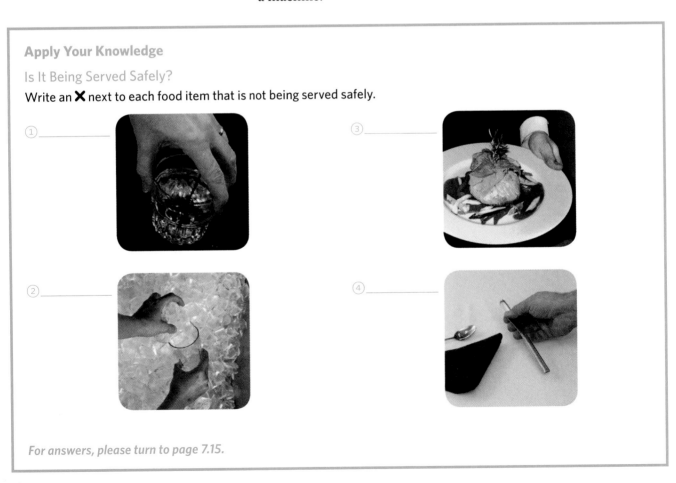

① _____

② _____

③ _____

④ _____

For answers, please turn to page 7.15.

Apply Your Knowledge

Re-serve or Throw Out?

Write a **T** next to the food that you must throw out. Write an **R** next to the items you can re-serve.

1 _____ Chili held without temperature control for 5 hours

2 _____ Previously served, but untouched, basket of bread

3 _____ Bottle of ketchup

4 _____ Untouched slice of pie with whipped cream returned by a customer

5 _____ Individually wrapped crackers

6 _____ Unwrapped butter served on a plate

7 _____ Mustard packets

8 _____ Ice used to hold cold food on a self-service area

9 _____ Breaded, baked fish returned by a customer who wanted broiled fish

10 _____ An apple that has been in a vending machine for 8 days that has been washed and wrapped

For answers, please turn to page 7.15.

Chapter Summary

- When holding TCS food for service, keep hot food at 135°F (57°C) or higher. Never use hot-holding equipment to reheat food. Keep cold food at 41°F (5°C) or lower. Check the internal temperature of food at least every four hours. Throw food out if it is not at the correct temperature.

- Review the guidelines for keeping food safe when holding food without temperature control.

- In general, staff should be trained to avoid bare-hand contact with ready-to-eat food. They should also learn to use separate utensils for serving different food items.

- Teach staff the correct ways for handling service items and tableware. Staff should also be trained on the potential hazards of re-serving food such as plate garnishes, breads, or open dishes of condiments.

- Self-service areas can be contaminated by staff and customers. Protect food on display with sneeze guards, packaging, or other tools designed to keep food safe. Post self-service rules. Make it clear to customers that clean plates must be used for refills. Put the correct labels on displayed food and bulk food available for self-service. Make sure equipment holds food at the correct temperature. Follow safety procedures when prepping, delivering, or serving food off-site.

- Vending machine food should be handled as carefully as any other food. Check product shelf life daily. Hold TCS food at the correct temperature.

Chapter Review Case Study

To keep food safe during holding and serving, you must know how to hold hot and cold food; use time as a method of control to hold food; and prevent contamination of food in self-service areas and when serving food to customers.

Now, take what you have learned in this chapter and apply it to the following case study.

Jill, a line cook on the morning shift at Memorial Hospital, was busy helping the kitchen staff put food on display for lunch in the hospital cafeteria. Ann, the kitchen manager who usually supervised lunch in the cafeteria, was at an all-day seminar on food safety. Jill was also responsible for making sure meals were trayed and put into food carts for transport to the patients' rooms. The staff also packed two dozen meals each day for a neighborhood group that delivered them to homebound elderly people.

First, Jill looked for insulated food containers for the delivery meals. When she could not find them, she loaded the meals into cardboard boxes she found near the back door, knowing the driver would arrive soon to pick them up. The lunch hour was hectic. The cafeteria was busy, and the staff had many meals to tray and deliver.

As the lunch period was ending, Jill breathed a sigh of relief. She moved down the cafeteria serving line, checking food temperatures. One of the casseroles was at 130°F (54°C). Jill checked the water level in the steam table and turned up the thermostat. She then went to clean up the kitchen and finish her shift.

① What did Jill do wrong?

_____

_____

_____

_____

_____

② What should Jill have done?

_____

_____

_____

_____

_____

_____

For answers, please turn to page 7.15.

Study Questions

Circle the best answer to each question.

1. **Which part of the plate should a food handler avoid touching when serving customers?**

   A Bottom

   B Edge

   C Side

   D Top

2. **An operation has a small salad bar with 8 different items on it. How many serving utensils are needed to serve the items on the salad bar?**

   A 2

   B 4

   C 6

   D 8

3. **At what maximum internal temperature should cold TCS food be held?**

   A 0°F (-17°C)

   B 32°F (0°C)

   C 41°F (5°C)

   D 60°F (16°C)

4. **What item must customers take each time they return to a self-service area for more food?**

   A Clean plate

   B Extra napkins

   C Hand sanitizer

   D New serving spoon

5. **At what minimum temperature should hot TCS food be held?**

   A 115°F (46°C)

   B 125°F (52° C)

   C 135°F (57 °C)

   D 145°F (63°C)

Continued on the next page ▶

▶ *Continued from previous page*

⑥ **An operation is located in a jurisdiction that allows it to hold TCS food without temperature control. How many hours can it display hot TCS food without temperature control before the food must be sold, served, or thrown out?**

A 2

B 4

C 6

D 8

⑦ **Which food items can be displayed in a self-service area without the use of packaging, sneeze guards, or a display case to protect them from contamination?**

A Bulk deli rolls

B Nuts in the shell

C Sushi-grade fish

D Cooked shrimp

⑧ **What is the maximum distance that sneeze guards can be located from the self-service counter to protect food from contamination?**

A 8 inches (20 cm)

B 10 inches (25 cm)

C 12 inches (30 cm)

D 14 inches (35 cm)

For answers, please turn to page 7.15.

Answers

7.4   Is It Being Handled Safely?

1, 3, and 4 should be marked. The soup in 1 should be held at 135°F (57°C) or higher. It is only being held at 120°F (49°C), which is unsafe. The potato salad in 3 is being held without temperature control, but the temperature has exceeded 70°F (21°C), which is unsafe. The soup in 4 is not being handled safely because it is being reheated in a hot-holding unit.

7.10   Is It Being Served Safely?

1, 2, 3, and 4 should be marked.

7.11   Re-serve or Throw Out?

① T   ⑥ T

② T   ⑦ R

③ R   ⑧ T

④ T   ⑨ T

⑤ R   ⑩ R

7.12   Chapter Review Case Study

① Here is what Jill did wrong.

- She packed the deliveries in cardboard boxes instead of food-grade, insulated containers.

- She failed to make sure that the internal temperature of the food on the steam table was checked at least every four hours. This would have alerted her to the fact that the steam table was not maintaining the correct temperature and that the casserole was in the temperature danger zone.

② Here is what Jill should have done.

- She should have kept the delivery meals in a hot-holding cabinet or left the food in a steam table until suitable containers were found or the driver arrived.

- She should have thrown out the casserole and any other food that was not at the correct temperature, because she did not know how long the food was in the temperature danger zone.

7.13   Study Questions

① D   ⑤ C

② D   ⑥ B

③ C   ⑦ B

④ A   ⑧ D

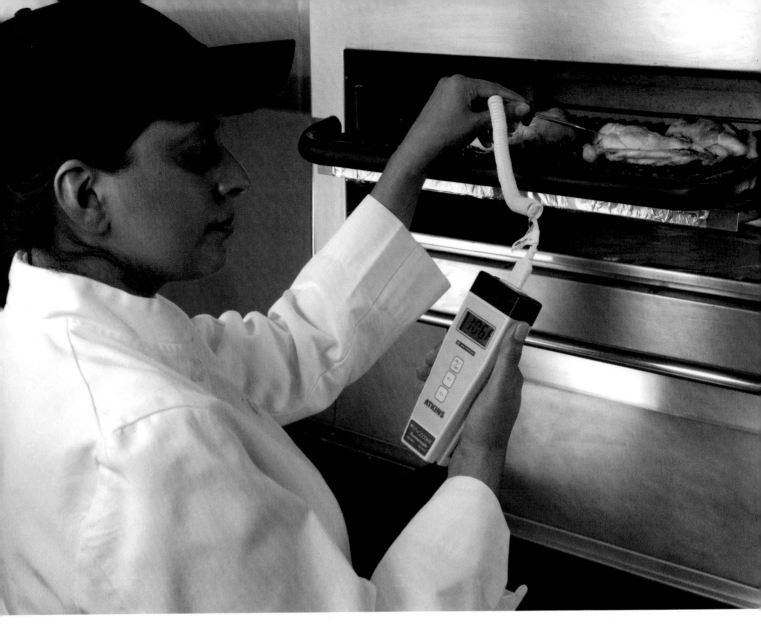

chapter 8
Food Safety Management Systems

Food Safety Management Systems

— Overview of Food Safety Management Systems
— Active Managerial Control
— HACCP

((NEWS)) Blue Skies Handles It Correctly

The calls started on a Thursday morning at Blue Skies Café, a small but well-liked diner in a busy city neighborhood. The callers complained of stomach cramps and diarrhea. The owner of the café took the first few calls and realized that she might have a foodborne-illness outbreak on her hands. She filled out an incident report for each call, and then she contacted the local regulatory authority.

"We were also getting calls, so we went to the café to see what happened," said the health inspector assigned to the case. "With the cooperation of the owner, we were able to identify the Caesar salad dressing as the source of the customers' illnesses."

A batch of the dressing was made with contaminated eggs. It eventually got 30 people sick. Because Caesar dressing isn't fully cooked, the café could not have done anything different to prep the dressing. "To correct the issue, we now use pasteurized eggs for the dressing, and we make new batches every few hours," said the owner.

The inspector also noted that the café's health-inspection score was not changed because of the outbreak. Nor was the operation forced to close. "They handled the problem quickly, and the rest of the operation is clean and well run," he said. Additionally, the café's insurance covered the healthcare costs and lost wages that the outbreak caused.

You Can Prevent This

A foodborne-illness outbreak is any manager's nightmare. But, as you can see in the story above, you can survive one. Creating a food safety management system will help prevent problems before they happen.

In this chapter, you will learn about the following systems.

- Food safety management systems

- Active managerial control

- Hazard Analysis Critical Control Point (HACCP)

Food Safety Management Systems

— Overview of Food Safety Management Systems
— Active Managerial Control
— HACCP

Food Safety Management Systems

In chapters 4 through 7, you learned how to handle food safely throughout the flow of food. Now, you will learn how all of it can be applied to a food safety management system. To do this, you must understand how a food safety management system works.

Overview of Food Safety Management Systems

A food safety management system is a group of practices and procedures intended to prevent foodborne illness. It does this by actively controlling risks and hazards throughout the flow of food.

Having some food safety programs already in place gives you the foundation for your system. The principles presented in the ServSafe program are the basis of these programs. Here are some examples of the programs your operation needs.

Personal hygiene program

Food safety training program

Supplier selection and specification program

Quality control and assurance programs

Cleaning and sanitation program

Standard operating procedures (SOPs)

ENRICO'S STANDARD OPERATING PROCEDURES

Facility design and equipment maintenance program

Pest-control program

Active Managerial Control

Earlier, you learned that there are five common risk factors for foodborne illness.

1 Purchasing food from unsafe sources

2 Failing to cook food correctly

3 Holding food at incorrect temperatures

4 Using contaminated equipment

5 Practicing poor personal hygiene

It is the manager's responsibility to actively control these and other risk factors for foodborne illness. This is called active managerial control. It is important to note that active managerial control is proactive rather than reactive. You must anticipate risks and plan for them.

There are many ways to achieve active managerial control in the operation. According to the Food and Drug Administration (FDA), you can use simple tools such as training programs, manager supervision, and the incorporation of SOPs. Active managerial control can also be achieved through more complex solutions such as a HACCP program.

Monitoring is critical to the success of active managerial control. Food will be safe if managers monitor critical activities in the operation. For example, the manager in the photo at left is monitoring a food handler as she carries out the critical task of cooling food correctly. Managers must also take the necessary corrective action when required. They must also verify that the actions taken to control the risk factors for foodborne illness are actually working.

Something to Think About...

Get a Handle on it!

A local regulatory authority was inspecting an operation in a large quick-service chain. The inspector noticed that the grill operator handling raw chicken fillets also put cooked fillets in a holding drawer. A sandwich maker touched the handle of the drawer each time she retrieved a cooked fillet.

The inspector saw that the grill operator was contaminating the holding-drawer handle. It happened each time he put a cooked fillet inside— since his hands had touched raw chicken. When the sandwich maker touched the contaminated handle, there was chance of cross-contamination.

Working with the manager, the inspector recommended adding an extra handle to the holding drawer. The grill operator and sandwich maker were assigned their own handle. The chain adopted the recommendation in all of its units.

In dealing with the risk of contamination, the chain practiced active managerial control. This included modifying their SOPs to control the risk and retraining staff. They also incorporated the new SOPs in the chain's monitoring program.

The FDA's Public Health Interventions

The FDA provides specific recommendations for controlling the common risk factors for foodborne illness. These are known as public health interventions. They are designed to protect public health.

Demonstration of knowledge   As a manager, you must be able to show that you know what to do to keep food safe. Becoming certified in food safety is one way to show this.

Staff health controls   Procedures must be put in place to make sure staff are practicing personal hygiene. For example, staff must know that they must report illnesses and illness symptoms to management.

Controlling hands as a vehicle of contamination   Controls must be put in place to prevent bare-hand contact with ready-to-eat food. This might include requiring the use of tongs to handle ready-to-eat food, as shown in the photo at left.

Time and temperature parameters for controlling pathogens
Procedures must be put in place to limit the time food spends in the temperature danger zone. Requiring food handlers to check the temperature of food being hot-held every two hours is an example.

Consumer advisories   Notices must be provided to customers if you serve raw or undercooked menu items. These notices must include a statement about the risks of eating these foods.

HACCP

There are many systems you can implement to achieve active managerial control of foodborne illness risk factors. Hazard Analysis Critical Control Point (HACCP) is one such system. HACCP (pronounced HASS-ip) is based on identifying significant biological, chemical, or physical hazards at specific points within a product's flow. Once identified, the hazards can be prevented, eliminated, or reduced to safe levels.

An effective HACCP system must be based on a written plan. This plan must be specific to each facility's menu, customers, equipment, processes, and operations. Since each HACCP plan is unique, a plan that works for one operation may not work for another.

The HACCP Approach

A HACCP plan is based on seven basic principles. They were created by the National Advisory Committee on Microbiological Criteria for Foods. These principles are the seven steps that outline how to create a HACCP plan.

The Seven HACCP Principles

Each HACCP principle builds on the information gained from the previous principle. You must consider all seven principles, in order, when developing your plan.

Here are the seven principles.

❶ Conduct a hazard analysis.

❷ Determine critical control points (CCPs).

❸ Establish critical limits.

❹ Establish monitoring procedures.

❺ Identify corrective actions.

❻ Verify that the system works.

❼ Establish procedures for record keeping and documentation.

In general terms, the principles break into three groups.

- Principles 1 and 2 help you identify and evaluate your hazards.
- Principles 3, 4, and 5 help you establish ways for controlling those hazards.
- Principles 6 and 7 help you maintain the HACCP plan and system, and verify its effectiveness.

The next few pages provide an introduction to these principles. They also present an overview of how to build a HACCP program.

A real-world example has also been included for each principle. It shows the efforts of Enrico's, an Italian restaurant, as it implements a HACCP program. The example will appear after the explanation of each principle.

Principle 1: Conduct a Hazard Analysis

First, identify and assess potential hazards in the food you serve. Start by looking at how food is processed in your operation. Many types of food are processed in similar ways. Here are some common processes.

- Prepping and serving without cooking (salads, cold sandwiches, etc.)
- Prepping and cooking for same-day service (grilled chicken sandwiches, hamburgers, etc.)
- Prepping, cooking, holding, cooling, reheating, and serving (chili, soup, pasta sauce with meat, etc.)

Look at your menu and identify items that are processed like this. Next, identify the TCS food. Determine where food safety hazards are likely to occur for each TCS food. There are many types of hazards to look for. These can come from biological, chemical, or physical contaminants.

The management team at Enrico's decided to implement a HACCP program. They began by analyzing their hazards.

The team noted that many of their dishes are received, stored, prepared, cooked, and served the same day. The most popular of these items was the spicy charbroiled chicken breast.

The team determined that bacteria were the most likely hazard to food prepared this way.

Principle 2: Determine Critical Control Points (CCPs)

Find the points in the process where the identified hazard(s) can be prevented, eliminated, or reduced to safe levels. These are the critical control points (CCPs). Depending on the process, there may be more than one CCP.

Principle 2 Example

Enrico's management identified cooking as the CCP for food prepared and cooked for immediate service. This included the chicken breasts.

These food items must be handled correctly throughout the flow of food. However, correct cooking is the only step that will eliminate or reduce bacteria to safe levels.

Since the chicken breasts were prepared for immediate service, cooking was the only CCP identified.

Principle 3: Establish Critical Limits

For each CCP, establish minimum or maximum limits. These limits must be met to prevent or eliminate the hazard, or to reduce it to a safe level.

Principle 3 Example

With cooking identified as the CCP for Enrico's chicken breasts, a critical limit was needed. Management determined that the critical limit would be cooking the chicken to a minimum internal temperature of 165°F (74°C) for 15 seconds.

They decided that the critical limit could be met by cooking chicken breasts in the broiler for 16 minutes.

Principle 4: Establish Monitoring Procedures

Once critical limits have been created, determine the best way for your operation to check them. Make sure the limits are consistently met. Identify who will monitor them and how often.

Principle 4 Example

At Enrico's, each charbroiled chicken breast is cooked to order. The team decided to check the critical limit by inserting a clean and sanitized thermocouple probe into the thickest part of each chicken breast.

The grill cook must check the temperature of each chicken breast after cooking. Each chicken breast must reach the minimum internal temperature of 165°F (74°C) for 15 seconds.

Principle 5: Identify Corrective Actions

Identify steps that must be taken when a critical limit is not met. These steps should be determined in advance.

Principle 5 Example

If the chicken breast has not reached its critical limit within the 16-minute cook time, the grill cook at Enrico's must keep cooking the chicken breast until it has reached it.

This and all other corrective actions are noted in the temperature log.

Principle 6: Verify That the System Works

Determine if the plan is working as intended. Evaluate it on a regular basis. Use your monitoring charts, records, hazard analysis, etc.; and determine if your plan prevents, reduces, or eliminates identified hazards.

Principle 6 Example

Enrico's management team performs HACCP checks once per shift. They make sure that critical limits were met and appropriate corrective actions were taken when needed.

They also check the temperature logs on a weekly basis to identify patterns. This helps to determine if processes or procedures need to be changed. For example, over several weeks they noticed problems toward the end of each week. The chicken breasts often failed to meet the critical limit. The appropriate corrective action was being taken.

Management discovered that Enrico's received chicken shipments from a different supplier on Thursdays. This supplier provided a six-ounce chicken breast. Enrico's chicken specifications listed a four-ounce chicken breast. Management worked with the supplier to ensure they received four-ounce breasts. The receiving procedures were changed to include a weight check.

Principle 7: Establish Procedures for Record Keeping and Documentation

Maintain your HACCP plan and keep all documentation created when developing it. Keep records for the following actions.

* Monitoring activities

* Taking corrective action

* Validating equipment (checking for good working condition)

* Working with suppliers (i.e., shelf-life studies, invoices, specifications, challenge studies, etc.)

Principle 7 Example

Enrico's management team determined that time-temperature logs should be kept for three months. Receiving invoices would be kept for 60 days. The team used this documentation to support and revise their HACCP plan

Another HACCP Example

The Enrico's example shows one type of HACCP plan. Another plan may look very different when it deals with food that is processed more simply. For example, food that is prepared and served without cooking needs a different approach.

Here is an example of the HACCP plan developed by The Fruit Basket. This fruit-only operation is known for its signature item—the Melon Medley salad.

1 Analyzing hazards   The HACCP team at The Fruit Basket decided to look at hazards for the Melon Medley. The salad has fresh watermelon, honeydew, and cantaloupe. The team determined that bacteria pose a risk to the fresh-cut melons.

2 Determining CCPs   The melons are prepped, held, and served without cooking. The team determined that preparation and holding are CCPs for the salad. They decided that cleaning and drying the melons' surfaces during prep, as shown in the photo at left, would reduce bacteria. Holding the melon at the correct temperature could prevent the bacteria's growth. Receiving was ruled out as a CCP, since the operation only purchases melons from approved suppliers.

3 Establishing critical limits   For the preparation CCP, the team decided the critical limit would be met by washing, scrubbing, and drying whole melons. They created an SOP with techniques for washing the melons. For the holding CCP, they decided that the salad must be held at 41°F (5°C) or lower, because it had cut melons.

4 Establishing monitoring procedures   The team decided that the operation's team leader should monitor the salad's critical limits. The team leader must observe food handlers to make sure they are prepping the melons the correct way. Food handlers must remove all surface dirt from the washed melons. Then they must cut, mix, and portion the salad into containers. The finished salads are put in the display cooler. The team leader must then monitor the temperature of the held salads to make sure the holding critical limit is met. The internal temperature of the salads must be 41°F (5°C) or lower. It must be checked three times per day, as shown in the photo at left.

5 Identifying corrective actions   Sometimes after preparation, the melons still have surface dirt. The team had to determine a corrective action for this. They decided that the action would be to rewash the melons. Then the team leader must approve the melons before they are sliced.

To correct a holding temperature that is higher than 41°F (5°C), the team leader must check the temperature of every Melon Medley in the cooler. Any salad that is above 41°F (5°C) must be thrown out.

6 Verifying that the system works   To make sure the system is working correctly, the team decided that the operation team leader must review the Manager Daily HACCP Check Sheet at the end of each shift. The team leader makes sure that each item was checked and initialed. The team leader also confirms that all corrective actions have been taken and recorded. The Fruit Basket also evaluates the HACCP system quarterly to see if it is working.

7 Establishing procedures for record keeping   Since a foodborne illness associated with fresh produce can take as long as 16 weeks to emerge, the team determined that all HACCP records must be maintained for 16 weeks and kept on file.

Specialized Processing Methods and HACCP

Some food processes are highly specialized and can be a serious health risk if specific procedures are not followed. Typically these processes are carried out at processing plants.

- Smoking food as a method to preserve it (but not to enhance flavor).

- Using food additives or adding components such as vinegar to preserve or alter it so it no longer requires time and temperature control for safety.

- Curing food.

- Custom-processing animals. For example, this may include dressing deer in the operation for personal use.

- Packaging food using reduced-oxygen packaging (ROP) methods. This includes MAP, vacuum-packed, and *sous vide* food. *Clostridium botulinum* and *Listeria monocytogenes* are risks to food packaged in these ways.

- Treating (e.g., pasteurizing) juice on-site, and packaging it for later sale.

- Sprouting seeds or beans.

A variance from the regulatory authority will be required before processing food this way. A variance is a document that allows a requirement to be waived or changed.

A HACCP plan may also be required if the processing method carries a higher risk of causing a foodborne illness. There may also be dangers unique to these processes that are best addressed by HACCP. For example, if not done correctly, reduced-oxygen packaging (ROP) has a very high risk of causing a foodborne illness. Because of this, a HACCP plan is required when a variance has not been requested.

Check with your local regulatory authority before using any of these specialized processing methods on-site.

Apply Your Knowledge

It's the Principle of the Thing

Identify the HACCP principle defined by each statement. Write the number of the principle in the space provided.

Ⓐ _____ Checking to see if critical limits are being met

Ⓑ _____ Keep HACCP plan documents

Ⓒ _____ Assessing risks within the flow of food

Ⓓ _____ Specific places in the flow of food where a hazard can be prevented, eliminated, or reduced to a safe level

Ⓔ _____ Predetermined step taken when a critical limit is not met

Ⓕ _____ Minimum or maximum boundaries that must be met to prevent a hazard

Ⓖ _____ Determining if the HACCP plan is working as intended

① Hazard analysis
② Critical control points
③ Critical limits
④ Monitoring
⑤ Corrective action
⑥ Verification
⑦ Record keeping and documentation

For answers, please turn to page 8.15.

Chapter Summary

- A food safety management system is a group of procedures and practices intended to prevent foodborne illness. It does this by actively controlling risks and hazards throughout the flow of food.

- It is the manager's responsibility to actively control the risk factors for foodborne illness. This is called active managerial control. It can be achieved by incorporating specific actions and procedures into the operation to prevent foodborne illness.

- The FDA provides specific recommendations for controlling the common risk factors for foodborne illness. These are known as public health interventions. They are designed to protect public health.

- HACCP is based on identifying significant biological, chemical, or physical hazards at specific points within a product's flow. Once identified, the hazards can be prevented, eliminated, or reduced to safe levels.

- A HACCP plan is based on seven basic principles. These principles are the seven steps that outline how to create a HACCP plan.

- Some food processes are highly specialized and can be a serious health risk if specific procedures are not followed. This includes processing methods such as curing food, or smoking food to extend shelf life. Always check with your local regulatory authority before using specialized processing methods on-site.

Chapter Review Case Study

You can address food safety risks in you operation by creating a food safety management system.

Now, take what you have learned in this chapter and apply it to the following case study.

Maria, an owner/operator of a family restaurant, realized that she needed to do more to keep her place safe. That meant taking charge of food safety in a more formal way than before. It was time to develop a food safety management system. Though she hadn't had any formal training in HACCP, she wanted to develop a HACCP plan for her operation.

Maria began by reviewing her menu to identify CCPs for each menu item. Most dishes on the menu were grilled items that were prepared, cooked, and then served. Maria determined that risks to these items could best be controlled through cooking, so she identified cooking as the CCP. Next, she identified critical limits for each CCP. For grilled hamburgers, she determined that cooking them to 150°F (66°C) for 15 seconds would reduce pathogens to a safe level. For grilled chicken, she knew it was necessary to cook it to 165°F (74°C) for 15 seconds.

Maria decided to monitor the critical limits by having cooks press on the meat with their fingertips to check for doneness. As an additional safeguard, she required cooks to cut open product to check the color for doneness. Maria knew she needed to identify a corrective action for products that had not been cooked enough. She decided that if the meat did not feel right, or if the color inside was not correct, cooks needed to keep cooking the meat.

Maria knew that record keeping was often part of a HACCP program, but she wasn't sure what types of records to keep. She ended up deciding that they really weren't necessary for her operation.

① What did Maria do correctly?

_____

_____

_____

② What mistakes did Maria make?

_____

_____

_____

For answers, please turn to page 8.15.

Study Questions

Circle the best answer to each question.

① **The temperature of a roast is checked to see if it has met its critical limit of 145°F (63°C) for 4 minutes. This is an example of which HACCP principle?**

A Verification

B Monitoring

C Record keeping

D Hazard analysis

② **The temperature of a pot of beef stew is checked during holding. The stew has not met the critical limit and is thrown out according to house policy. Throwing out the stew is an example of which HACCP principle?**

A Monitoring

B Verification

C Hazard analysis

D Corrective action

③ **The deli serves cold sandwiches in a self-serve display. Which step in the flow of food would be a critical control point?**

A Storage

B Cooling

C Cooking

D Reheating

④ **What is the first step in developing a HACCP plan?**

A Identify corrective actions.

B Conduct a hazard analysis.

C Establish monitoring procedures.

D Determine critical control points.

⑤ **What is the purpose of a food safety management system?**

A Keep all areas of the facility clean and pest free

B Identify, tag, and repair faulty equipment within the facility

C Identify and control possible hazards throughout the flow of food

D Document and use the correct methods for purchasing and receiving food

Continued on the next page ▶

▶ *Continued from previous page*

⑥ **Reviewing temperature logs and other records to make sure that the HACCP plan is working as intended is an example of which HACCP principle?**

A Monitoring

B Verification

C Hazard analysis

D Record keeping

⑦ **A chef sanitized a thermometer probe and then checked the temperature of minestrone soup being held in a hot-holding unit. The temperature was 120°F (49°C), which did not meet the operation's critical limit of 135°F (57°C). The chef recorded the temperature in the log and reheated the soup to 165°F (74°C) for 15 seconds. Which was the corrective action?**

A Reheating the soup

B Checking the critical limit

C Sanitizing the thermometer probe

D Recording the temperature in the log

⑧ **What does an operation that wants to smoke food as a method of preservation need to have before processing food this way?**

A Food safety certificate

B Crisis-management plan

C Master cleaning schedule

D Variance from the local regulatory authority

For answers, please turn to page 8.15.

Answer Key

8.11 It's the Principle of the Thing

Ⓐ 4 Ⓔ 5

Ⓑ 7 Ⓕ 3

Ⓒ 1 Ⓖ 6

Ⓓ 2

8.12 Chapter Review Case Study

① Maria did the following correctly.

- Maria was correct in her decision to develop a food safety management system. This is the best way to address food safety risks in her operation.

- Maria was correct in assuming that cooking was a CCP for the grilled items.

② Maria made the following mistakes.

- Maria should have started by conducting a hazard analysis. It is important to determine all of the places where food safety hazards are likely to occur.

- Maria needed to look for more than just biological hazards because hazards can also be chemical or physical.

- The critical limit for the hamburgers was not correct. The temperature needed to be 155°F (68°C) or higher for 15 seconds.

- There are problems with the way that Maria planned to monitor her critical limits. The only way to determine whether food has been cooked to the correct internal temperature is to check the product using an approved thermometer.

- Maria should have planned to develop temperature logs that could be used to record the internal temperature of the grilled meat and poultry at regular intervals. These records could then be used to help determine whether Maria's HACCP plan was working as intended, which is called verification.

8.13 Study Questions

① B ⑤ C

② D ⑥ B

③ A ⑦ A

④ B ⑧ D

chapter 9
Safe Facilities and Pest Management

Interior Requirements for a Safe Operation	Emergencies That Affect the Facility	Pest Management
— Floors, Walls, and Ceilings — Utilities and Building Systems — Maintaining the Facility		— Pest Prevention — Pest Control

((NEWS)) Operation Closes to Fix Health Code Violations

A foodservice operation located on old Route 66 was closed by the local regulatory authority. A long list of violations was cited by the inspector. The operation, which opened its doors in the 1940s, was infested with roaches in both storage areas. Food was unprotected from potential sources of contamination during storage, preparation, and service. It was also discovered that the operation had been using old, broken equipment, and the building was in disrepair. Several pieces of equipment were being held together with duct tape, and some tabletop equipment was in such disrepair that the inspector told the operator to throw it out immediately.

The long-time owners said that they and their managers were fully committed to implementing the inspector's recommendations to bring their operation up to state and local codes. They also apologized to their loyal customers in a full-page ad in the local newspaper. They pledged to work hard at running a clean and safe operation to win back their customers.

You Can Prevent This

Broken, outdated equipment and a building in disrepair can lead to contamination, no matter how clean an operation is. To make sure your facility is safe for foodservice, you should know the following.

- How to pick materials and equipment that are safe for use in foodservice operations

- How to install and maintain equipment

- How to avoid food safety hazards caused by utilities

- How to maintain your facility

- How to handle emergencies

- How to prevent and control pests

Interior Requirements for a Safe Operation	Emergencies That Affect the Facility	Pest Management
— Floors, Walls, and Ceilings — Utilities and Building Systems — Maintaining the Facility		— Pest Prevention — Pest Control

Interior Requirements for a Safe Operation

The materials, equipment, and utilities in your operation play a part in keeping food safe. Given the opportunity, you should choose these items with food safety in mind.

Floors, Walls, and Ceilings

When choosing flooring, wall, and ceiling materials, pick those that are smooth and durable. This makes cleaning easier.

Once installed, flooring, walls, and ceilings must be regularly maintained. Replace missing or broken ceiling tiles. Do the same for flooring. Repair all holes in walls.

Equipment Selection

Foodservice equipment must meet certain standards if it will come in contact with food. NSF is an organization that creates these national standards. NSF is accredited by the American National Standards Institute (ANSI). NSF/ANSI standards for food equipment require that it be nonabsorbent, smooth, and corrosion resistant. Food equipment must also be easy to clean, durable, and resistant to damage.

Installing and Maintaining Equipment

Stationary equipment should be easy to clean and easy to clean around. In the photo at left, the dishwasher is installed so that the floor can be cleaned easily.

When installing equipment, follow the manufacturer's recommendations. Also, check with your regulatory authority for requirements. In general, stationary equipment should be installed as follows.

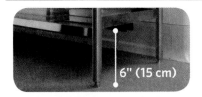

Floor-mounted equipment   Put floor-mounted equipment on legs at least 6 inches (15 centimeters) high. Another option is to seal it to a masonry base.

Tabletop equipment   Put tabletop equipment on legs at least 4 inches (10 centimeters) high. Or, seal it to the countertop.

Once you have installed equipment, make sure it is maintained regularly by qualified people. Also, set up a maintenance schedule with your supplier or manufacturer. Check equipment regularly to be sure it is working correctly.

Dishwashing Machines

Dishwashers vary by size, style, and sanitizing method. For example, some sanitize with very hot water. Others use a chemical solution.

Consider these guidelines when selecting and installing dishwashers.

Installation   Dishwashers must be installed so that they are reachable and conveniently located. That installation must also keep utensils, equipment, and other food-contact surfaces from becoming contaminated. Always follow the manufacturer's instructions when installing, operating, and maintaining dishwashers.

Supplies   Use detergents and sanitizers approved by the local regulatory authority.

Settings   Purchase dishwashers that have the ability to measure the following.

- Water temperature
- Water pressure
- Cleaning and sanitizing chemical concentration

Information about the correct settings should be posted on the machine. The label in the photo at left shows an example.

Cleaning   Clean dishwashers as often as necessary. Follow the manufacturer's recommendations and local regulatory requirements.

Three-Compartment Sinks

Many operations use three-compartment sinks to clean and sanitize items manually in the operation. Purchase sinks that are large enough to accommodate large equipment and utensils. You should also have other methods for cleaning these items, such as cleaning them in place.

HOT WATER SANITIZING
WASH TEMPERATURE 160°F (71°C) MIN.
FINAL RINSE TEMP 180°F (82°C) MIN.
BLDG. SUPPLY FLOW PRESS. 20±5 P.S.I.
MAX. CONVEYOR SPEED 6.2 FT./MINUTE

How This Relates to Me

What types of dishwashers are allowed in your jurisdiction?

_____

_____

_____

_____

Handwashing Stations

Handwashing stations should be put in areas that make it easy for staff to wash their hands often. These stations are required in restrooms or directly next to them. Handwashing stations are also required in areas used for food prep, service, and dishwashing. Handwashing sinks must be used only for handwashing and not for any other purpose.

Make sure these stations work correctly and are well stocked and maintained. They must also be available at all times. Handwashing stations cannot be blocked by portable equipment or stacked full of dirty kitchenware. An example of this is shown in the photo at left. A handwashing station must have the following items.

Hot and cold running water   The water must be drinkable and meet temperature and pressure requirements.

Soap   The soap can be liquid, bar, or powder.

A way to dry hands   Disposable paper towels or a continuous towel system that supplies the user with a clean towel can be used. Hands can also be dried with a hand dryer using either warm air or room-temperature air delivered at high velocity.

Garbage container   Garbage containers are required if disposable paper towels are used.

Signage   A clearly visible sign or poster must tell staff to wash hands before returning to work. The message should be in all languages used by staff in the operation.

Some jurisdictions allow the use of automatic handwashing facilities in an operation. Check with your local regulatory authority for more information.

Utilities and Building Systems

An operation uses many utilities and building systems. Utilities include water, electricity, gas, sewage, and garbage disposal. Building systems include plumbing, lighting, and ventilation. There must be enough utilities to meet the needs of the operation. In addition, the utilities and systems must work correctly. If they do not, the risk of contamination is greater.

Water and Plumbing

Each regulatory authority establishes standards for water in their jurisdiction. Only water that is drinkable can be used for the preparation of food and come in contact with food-contact surfaces. This water may come from the following sources.

* Approved public water mains

* Private water sources that are regularly tested and maintained

* Closed, portable water containers

* Water transport vehicles

Regardless of where your water comes from, you should know how to prevent plumbing issues that can affect food safety.

Installation and maintenance   Plumbing that is not installed or maintained correctly can allow drinkable and unsafe water to be mixed. This can cause foodborne-illness outbreaks. Have only licensed plumbers work on the plumbing in your operation, as shown in the photo at left.

Cross-connection   The greatest challenge to water safety comes from cross-connections. A cross-connection is a physical link between safe water and dirty water, which can come from drains, sewers, or other wastewater sources.

A cross-connection is dangerous because it can let backflow occur. Backflow is the reverse flow of contaminants through a cross-connection into a drinkable water supply. Backflow can be the result of pressure pushing contaminants back into the water supply. It can also happen when high water use in one area of an operation creates a vacuum in the plumbing system that sucks contaminants back into the water supply. This is called backsiphonage. A running faucet below the flood rim of a sink is an example of a cross-connection that can lead to backsiphonage. A running hose in a mop bucket is another example, as shown in the illustration at left.

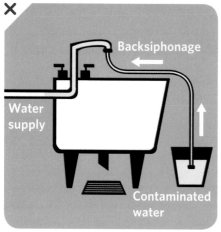

Backflow prevention   The best way to prevent backflow is to avoid creating a cross-connection. Do **NOT** attach a hose to a faucet unless a backflow prevention device is attached. A vacuum breaker is a mechanical device that prevents backsiphonage. It does this by closing a check valve and sealing the water supply line shut when water flow is stopped.

Other mechanical devices are used to prevent backflow. These include double check valve and reduced pressure zone backflow preventers. These devices include more than one check valve for sealing off the water supply. They also provide a way to determine if the check valves are operational.

Backflow prevention devices must be checked periodically to make sure they are working correctly. This must be done by a trained and certified technician. And, the work must be documented. Always follow local requirements and manufacturer's recommendations.

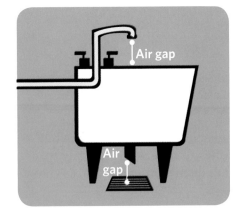

The only sure way to prevent backflow is to create an air gap. An air gap is an air space that separates a water supply outlet from a potentially contaminated source. A sink that is correctly designed and installed usually has two air gaps, as shown in the graphic at left. One is between the faucet and the flood rim of the sink. The other is between the drainpipe of the sink and the floor drain of the operation.

Lighting

Good lighting makes it easier to clean things in your operation. It also provides a safer environment.

Lighting intensity—how bright the lights are in the operation—is usually measured in units called foot-candles or lux. Different areas of the facility have different lighting intensity requirements. Local jurisdictions usually require prep areas to be brighter than other areas. This allows staff to recognize the condition of food. It also allows staff to identify items that need cleaning.

Once the appropriate level of lighting has been installed in each area of the facility, you must monitor it. Replace any bulbs that have burned out. And, make sure they are the correct size. All lights should have shatter-resistant lightbulbs or protective covers. These products prevent broken glass from contaminating food or food-contact surfaces.

Ventilation

Ventilation improves the air inside an operation. It removes heat, steam, and smoke from cooking lines. It also eliminates fumes and odors. If ventilation systems are not working correctly, grease and condensation will build up on walls and ceilings.

To prevent this, ventilation systems must be cleaned and maintained according to manufacturer's recommendations and/or local regulatory requirements.

Garbage

Garbage can attract pests and contaminate food, equipment, and utensils if not handled correctly. To control contamination from garbage, consider the following.

Garbage removal   Garbage should be removed from prep areas as quickly as possible to prevent odors, pests, and possible contamination. Staff must be careful when removing garbage so they do not contaminate food or food-contact surfaces. The food handler in the photo at left has not been careful and may contaminate the prep table.

Cleaning of containers   Clean the inside and outside of garbage containers frequently. This will help prevent the contamination of food and food-contact surfaces. It will also reduce odors and pests. Do **NOT** clean garbage containers near prep or food-storage areas.

Indoor containers   Containers must be leak proof, waterproof, and pest proof. They also should be easy to clean. Containers must be covered when not in use.

Designated storage areas   Waste and recyclables must be stored separately from food and food-contact surfaces. The storage of these items must not create a nuisance or a public health hazard.

Outdoor containers   Place garbage containers on a surface that is smooth, durable, and nonabsorbent. Asphalt and concrete are good choices, as shown in the photo at left. Make sure the containers have tight-fitting lids and are kept covered at all times. Keep their drain plugs in place.

Maintaining the Facility

Poor maintenance can cause food safety problems in your operation. To prevent problems, do the following.

- Clean the operation on a regular basis.

- Make sure all building systems work and are checked regularly.

- Make sure the building is sound. There should be no leaks, holes, or cracks in the floors, foundation, ceilings, or windows. In the photo at left, the maintenance worker is filling a crack in the wall to keep pests out.

- Control pests.

- Maintain the outside of the building correctly, including patios and parking lots.

Apply Your Knowledge

What's Missing?

The handwashing station is missing 3 items. What are they?

① _____

② _____

③ _____

For answers, please turn to page 9.17.

Apply Your Knowledge

What's Wrong with This Picture?

Write an ✗ next to the statement that best describes what the food handler has done wrong in the picture below.

① _____   He has created an air gap.

② _____   He has created a grease trap.

③ _____   He has created a vacuum breaker.

④ _____   He has created a cross-connection.

Which Sink?

Write an ✗ next to the sink where backsiphonage could occur.

① _____   ② _____

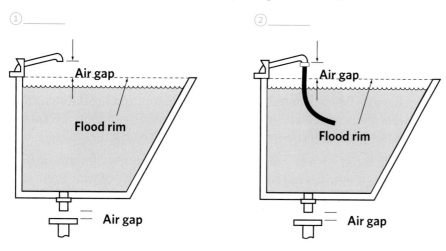

Garbage In, Garbage Out

Write an ✗ next to each unsafe practice when handling garbage and garbage containers.

① _____   Marvin cleans a garbage can on the floor drain grate, which is next to the steam-jacketed kettle.

② _____   Barry stacks garbage bags next to the prep table because he wants to take them out all at once.

③ _____   Ron sets garbage bags on the asphalt next to the Dumpster and then throws each bag inside.

④ _____   Michelle throws empty cans into the recycling container, which is stored in the prep area.

⑤ _____   Tunya throws an overcooked chicken breast into the open garbage can next to the sandwich line.

For answers, please turn to page 9.17.

Interior Requirements for a Safe Operation	Emergencies That Affect the Facility	Pest Management
— Floors, Walls, and Ceilings — Utilities and Building Systems — Maintaining the Facility		— Pest Prevention — Pest Control

Emergencies That Affect the Facility

Certain crises can affect the safety of the food you serve. Some of the most common include electrical power outages, fire, flooding, and sewage backups. These are considered by the local regulatory authority to be imminent health hazards. An imminent health hazard is a significant threat or danger to health that requires immediate correction or closure to prevent injury.

Other threats should also be considered.

Temperature control   Power failures and refrigeration breakdowns can threaten your ability to control the temperature of TCS food. This can result in the growth of pathogens.

Physical security   Unauthorized people inside a facility are a risk to food safety. This is especially true when they can access storage and processing areas. Also, acts of nature can weaken a facility's security.

Drinkable water supply   Threats to the drinkable water supply must also be considered. Broken water mains and breakdowns at water treatment facilities are a risk to the safety of food. Terrorist contamination of the water supply could also be a threat.

When faced with any of these crises, you must first determine if there is a significant risk to the safety or security of your food. If the risk is significant, service must be stopped. Then the local regulatory authority must be notified.

Spoiled or contaminated food must be thrown out, along with food in packaging that is not intact. Finally, you must decide how to correct the problem. Actions might include establishing time-temperature control of TCS food or cleaning and sanitizing surfaces in the operation. It might also include reestablishing the physical security of the operation. Or, verifying that the water supply is drinkable. Regardless, you will need approval from the local regulatory authority before continuing service.

How This Relates to Me

What are the local regulatory requirements in your jurisdiction when water service has been disrupted?

_____

_____

_____

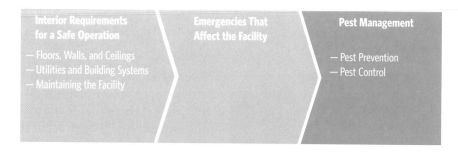

Interior Requirements for a Safe Operation	Emergencies That Affect the Facility	Pest Management
— Floors, Walls, and Ceilings — Utilities and Building Systems — Maintaining the Facility		— Pest Prevention — Pest Control

Pest Management

Rodents, insects, and other pests are more than just unsightly to customers. They can damage food, supplies, and facilities. But the greatest danger comes from their ability to spread diseases, including foodborne illnesses.

Pest Prevention

Prevention is critical in pest control. Follow these three basic rules to keep your operation pest free.

❶ Deny pests access to the operation.

❷ Deny pests food, water, and shelter.

❸ Work with a licensed pest control operator (PCO).

Deny access   Pests can be brought inside with deliveries or through building openings. Follow these guidelines to prevent this.

- Check all deliveries before they enter your operation. Refuse shipments in which you find pests or signs of pests. This includes egg cases and body parts (legs, wings, etc.).

- Make sure all of the points where pests can access the building are secure. Screen all windows and vents, and patch or replace them when needed. Seal cracks in floors and walls and around pipes, as shown in the photo at left. Install air curtains (also called air doors or fly fans) above or alongside doors.

Deny shelter   Careful cleaning eliminates the pests' food supply and destroys insect eggs. It also reduces the places pests can take shelter. Follow these guidelines to deny pests food and shelter.

- Throw out garbage quickly and correctly. Keep garbage containers clean and in good condition. Keep outdoor containers tightly covered. Clean up spills around garbage containers immediately, and wash containers regularly.

- Store recyclables in clean, pest-proof containers. Keep them as far away from your building as local regulations allow.

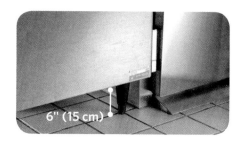

6" (15 cm)

- Store all food and supplies correctly and as quickly as possible. Keep food and supplies away from walls and at least six inches (15 centimeters) off the floor, as shown in the photo at left. Use FIFO to rotate products, so that pests do not have time to settle into them and breed.

- Clean up food and beverage spills immediately, including crumbs and scraps.

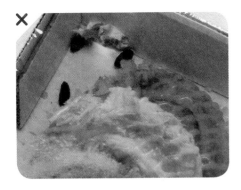

Pest Control

Even after you have made every effort to keep pests out, they may still get into your operation. If this happens, you must work with a PCO to get them under control. Even if you only spot a few pests, they may actually be present in large numbers. This is an infestation and can be very difficult to eliminate. Pests leave signs, letting you know they are there. Look for feces, nests, and damage on products, packaging, and the facility itself. An example of rodent damage to a package of Danish pastries is shown in the photo at left. Contact your PCO immediately if you see these, or any other pest-related problems, so that control measures can be taken.

Apply Your Knowledge

Keep 'Em Out!

Write an ✗ next to each situation that can lead to a pest infestation.

1. _____ Food in the dry-storage room is stored against the wall and 6 inches off the floor.

2. _____ Air curtains are installed around the back door of a kitchen.

3. _____ Recyclables are stored overnight in a clean container in the kitchen.

4. _____ Food is rotated during storage so that the oldest products are used first.

5. _____ A Dumpster is left open during the day to let it air out.

6. _____ A delivery driver brings a food delivery into the kitchen to be inspected.

7. _____ A food delivery is rejected because it contains moth wings.

8. _____ A kitchen has window screens with small holes in them.

For answers, please turn to page 9.17.

Chapter Summary

- Choose flooring, wall, and ceiling materials that are smooth and durable. This will make cleaning easier. Replace and maintain these materials when necessary.

- Make sure equipment that will come in contact with food is smooth, nonabsorbent, and easy to clean. Floor-mounted equipment must be put on legs at least six inches high or sealed to a masonry base. Tabletop equipment must be put on legs at least four inches high or sealed to the countertop.

- Dishwashing machines must be installed so that they prevent contamination of utensils, equipment, and other food-contact surfaces.

- Handwashing stations should include hot and cold running drinkable water, soap, and a way to dry hands. They should also include a garbage container if paper towels are provided, and signage reminding staff to wash hands before returning to work.

- Plumbing must always be installed and maintained by a licensed plumber. This will help prevent cross-connections from occurring. A cross-connection is dangerous because it can let backflow occur. Backflow is the reverse flow of contaminants through a cross-connection into a drinkable water supply.

- Garbage must be removed from prep areas as quickly as possible to prevent odors, pests, and possible contamination. Garbage containers must be leak proof, waterproof and pest proof. They must be cleaned, inside and out, frequently. Facilities must also be regularly maintained. Clean them on a regular basis, and make sure there are no leaks, holes, or cracks in the floors, foundation, or ceilings.

- To keep your operation pest free, you must deny pests access to the operation. You can do this by inspecting deliveries before they come into your operation. You also need to eliminate points of access. Deny pests access to food, water, and shelter.

Chapter Review Activities

Many parts of an operation's facility and equipment affect food safety. These include the materials and equipment used; equipment installation and maintenance; utilities and building systems; and facility maintenance.

Now, take what you have learned in this chapter and apply it to the following case studies.

1. Julio is the assistant manager of the staff cafeteria at The Vicor Company. When he came in this morning, he found that raw sewage had backed up through the floor drain near the freezers. How should he handle this problem?

2. Anita is an area supervisor for a small quick-service chain. On her first visit to one of the operations she noticed a buildup of grease on the kitchen walls. What should she direct the manager to do to fix this problem and make sure it does not happen again?

3. Jon is the manager of a small, family-owned, casual-dining operation. Since he started work six months ago, there have been some problems with the plumbing. The sinks have been draining more and more slowly. Also, each time the dishwasher finishes a cycle, a small puddle of water backs up onto the floor under the machine. What can Jon do to fix these problems?

For answers, please turn to page 9.17.

Study Questions

Circle the best answer to each question.

1 **What are the most important food safety features to look for when selecting flooring, wall, and ceiling materials?**

A Absorbent and durable

B Hard and durable

C Porous and durable

D Smooth and durable

2 **What organization creates national standards for foodservice equipment?**

A CDC

B EPA

C FDA

D NSF

3 **When installing tabletop equipment on legs, the space between the base of the equipment and the tabletop must be at least**

A 2 inches (5 centimeters).

B 4 inches (10 centimeters).

C 6 inches (15 centimeters).

D 8 inches (20 centimeters).

4 **Besides information on chemical concentration and water temperature, what other machine setting information should be posted on dishwashing machines?**

A Water pH

B Water salinity

C Water pressure

D Water hardness

5 **Signage posted at a handwashing station must include a reminder to staff to**

A wash hands before returning to work.

B use hot running water when washing.

C scrub hands and arms for 10 to 15 seconds.

D avoid touching faucet handles after washing.

6 **What is the only completely reliable method for preventing backflow?**

A Air gap

B Ball valve

C Cross-connection

D Vacuum breaker

Continued on the next page ▶

▶ *Continued from previous page*

⑦ **A food handler drops the end of a hose into a mop bucket and turns the water on to fill it. What has the food handler done wrong?**

A Created a cross-connection

B Created an air gap separation

C Prevented backflow

D Prevented atmospheric vacuuming

⑧ **Which area of the operation is usually required to be the brightest?**

A Dry-storage

B Preparation

C Refrigerated-storage

D Service

⑨ **An operation has a buildup of grease and condensation on the walls and ceiling. What is the most likely problem?**

A The ventilation system is not working correctly.

B The cleaning chemicals are not being used correctly.

C The staff are not cleaning the walls correctly.

D The grill is not being operated at a high-enough temperature.

⑩ **An operation received a violation in the outside area of the facility. The manager reviewed the area and saw that the Dumpster was placed on a freshly graveled drive. The lids were closed, and the drain plug was in place to prevent the Dumpster from draining. What was the problem?**

A The Dumpster lids should have been open to allow it to air out.

B The drain plug should have been removed to allow the Dumpster to drain correctly.

C The surface underneath the Dumpster should have been paved with concrete or asphalt.

D The Dumpster should have been freshly painted so that food debris would not stick to surfaces.

⑪ **A broken water main has caused the water in an operation to appear brown. What should the manager do?**

A Boil the water for 1 minute before use.

B Contact the local regulatory authority before use.

C Use the water for everything except dishwashing.

D Use the water for everything except handwashing.

⑫ **What is the best way to eliminate pests that have entered the operation?**

A Raise the heat in the operation after-hours.

B Lower the heat in the operation after-hours.

C Work with a licensed pest control operator (PCO).

D Apply over-the-counter pesticides around the operation.

For answers, please turn to page 9.17.

Answers

9.8   What's Missing?

① Soap

② Sign stating that staff must wash hands before returning to work

③ Garbage container for used paper towels

9.9   What's Wrong with This Picture?

4 should be marked. By submerging the hose in the bucket of water, the cross-connection can contaminate the drinkable water supply if pressure were to drop in the supply line.

9.9   Which Sink?

Sink 2 should be marked. The hose attached to the sink faucet has created a cross-connection. Backsiphonage could occur because the hose has been submerged in the sink water.

9.9   Garbage In, Garbage Out

1, 2, and 4 should be marked. Marvin should not have cleaned the container next to the kettle because it is used to prep food and could have become contaminated. Barry should not have stacked the garbage bags next to the prep table because this could have contaminated it. The recyclable container that Michelle used should not have been stored in the prep area. These containers should be stored separately from food and food-contact surfaces.

9.12   Keep 'Em Out!

1, 3, 5, 6, and 8 should be marked.

9.14   Chapter Review Activities

① Julio must first determine whether there is a significant risk to the safety of the food in his operation. If the risk is not significant, he must immediately correct the problem. If there is a significant risk to the safety of food, service must be stopped. Then Julio must contact the local regulatory authority. Once the problem has been fixed and the necessary cleanup performed, Julio will need approval from the local regulatory authority before continuing service.

② The ventilation system is not working correctly. Anita should ask the manager to schedule a service call to check the ventilation system. She should also ask the manager to have the ventilation system cleaned regularly following manufacturer's recommendations and local requirements.

③ Jon needs to contact a licensed plumber to fix the problem.

9.15   Study Questions

① D	④ C	⑦ A	⑩ C
② D	⑤ A	⑧ B	⑪ B
③ B	⑥ A	⑨ A	⑫ C

chapter 10
Cleaning and Sanitizing

Cleaning and Sanitizing	Dishwashing	Cleaning and Sanitizing in the Operation
— Cleaners — Sanitizers — How and When to Clean and Sanitize	— Machine Dishwashing — Manual Dishwashing — Storing Tableware and Equipment	— Cleaning the Premises — Cleaning Tools and Supplies — Developing a Cleaning Program

((NEWS)) Incorrectly Cleaned Yogurt Machine Makes Soldiers Sick

Several soldiers and their family members got sick at a military base in the northeastern United States. The victims had eaten frozen yogurt at a popular snack bar on the base. They suffered from vomiting, diarrhea, and chills. A child was admitted to the base hospital for severe dehydration.

An investigation showed that the yogurt machine was the culprit. It seems that food handlers at the snack bar did not break down the machine before cleaning it. They also failed to sanitize surfaces after cleaning them. This led to the outbreak. The local regulatory authority worked with the snack bar manager to put procedures in place to prevent any future incidents.

You Can Prevent This

In the story you just read, people got sick because the operation did not clean and sanitize equipment correctly. Cleaning and sanitizing food-contact surfaces can help you avoid foodborne-illness outbreaks. To do it correctly, you need to know about the following topics.

- The different methods of sanitizing and how to make sure they are effective

- How and when to clean and sanitize surfaces

- How to wash items in a dishwasher or a three-compartment sink and then store them

- How to use and store cleaning tools and supplies

- How to develop a cleaning program

Cleaning and Sanitizing	Dishwashing	Cleaning and Sanitizing in the Operation
— Cleaners — Sanitizers — How and When to Clean and Sanitize	— Machine Dishwashing — Manual Dishwashing — Storing Tableware and Equipment	— Cleaning the Premises — Cleaning Tools and Supplies — Developing a Cleaning Program

Cleaning and Sanitizing

Food can easily be contaminated if you don't keep your facility and equipment clean and sanitized. Cleaning removes food and other dirt from a surface. Sanitizing reduces pathogens on a surface to safe levels.

Cleaners

Cleaners must be stable, noncorrosive, and safe to use. Ask your supplier to help you pick cleaners that meet your needs. To use cleaners correctly, follow these guidelines.

- Follow manufacturers' instructions carefully, as the manager in the photo at left is doing. If not used the correct way, cleaners may not work and can even be dangerous.

- Do NOT use one type of cleaner in place of another unless the intended use is the same.

Sanitizers

Food-contact surfaces must be sanitized after they have been cleaned and rinsed. This can be done by using heat or chemicals.

Heat Sanitizing

One way to sanitize items is to soak them in hot water. For this method to work, the water must be at least 171°F (77°C). The items must be soaked for at least 30 seconds. Another way to sanitize items is to run them through a high-temperature dishwasher.

Chemical Sanitizing

Tableware, utensils, and equipment can be sanitized by soaking them in a chemical sanitizing solution. Or you can rinse, swab, or spray them with sanitizing solution, as shown in the photo at left.

Three common types of chemical sanitizers are chlorine, iodine, and quaternary ammonium compounds, or quats. Chemical sanitizers are regulated by state and federal environmental protection agencies (EPAs). For requirements, check with your local regulatory authority.

In some cases, you can use detergent-sanitizer blends to sanitize. Operations that have two-compartment sinks often use these. If you use a detergent-sanitizer blend, use it once to clean. Then use it a second time to sanitize.

Sanitizer Effectiveness

Several factors influence the effectiveness of chemical sanitizers. The most critical include concentration, temperature, contact time, water hardness, and pH.

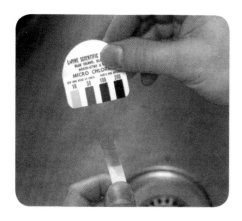

Concentration   Sanitizer solution is a mix of chemical sanitizer and water. The concentration of this mix—the amount of sanitizer to water—is critical. Too little sanitizer may make the solution weak and useless. Too much sanitizer may make the solution too strong and unsafe. It can also leave a bad taste on items or corrode metal.

Concentration is measured in parts per million (ppm). To check the concentration of a sanitizer solution, use a test kit, as shown in the photo at left. Make sure it is made for the sanitizer being used. These kits are usually available from the chemical manufacturer or supplier.

Hard water, food bits, and leftover detergent can reduce the solution's effectiveness. Change the solution when it looks dirty or its concentration is too low. Check the concentration often.

Temperature   The water in sanitizing solution must be the correct temperature. Follow manufacturers' recommendations.

Contact time   For a sanitizer solution to kill pathogens, it must make contact with the object being sanitized for a specific amount of time. The bain in the photo at left is being sanitized in an iodine sanitizing solution. It must be in contact with the solution for at least 30 seconds.

Water hardness   Water hardness can affect how well a sanitizer works. Water hardness is the amount of minerals in your water. Find out what your water hardness is from your municipality. Then work with your supplier to identify the correct amount of sanitizer to use for your water.

pH   Water pH can also affect a sanitizer. Find out what the pH of your water is from your municipality. Then work with your supplier to find out the correct amount of sanitizer to use for your water.

General Guidelines for the Effective Use of Chlorine, Iodine, and Quats

	Chlorine		Iodine	Quats
Water temperature	≥100°F (38°C)	≥75°F (24°C)	68°F (20°C)	75°F (24°C)
Water pH	≤10	≤8	≤5 or as per manufacturer's recommendation	As per manufacturer's recommendation
Water hardness	As per manufacturer's recommendation		As per manufacturer's recommendation	≤500 ppm or as per manufacturer's recommendation
Sanitizer concentration	50-99 ppm	50-99 ppm	12.5-25 ppm	As per manufacturer's recommendation
Sanitizer contact time	≥7 sec	≥7 sec	≥30 sec	≥30 sec

How and When to Clean and Sanitize

All surfaces must be cleaned and rinsed. This includes walls, storage shelves, and garbage containers. However, any surface that touches food, such as knives, stockpots, cutting boards, or prep tables, must be cleaned and sanitized.

How to clean and sanitize   To clean and sanitize a surface, follow these steps.

1 Scrape or remove food bits from the surface.

- Use the correct cleaning tool, such as a nylon brush or pad, or a cloth towel.

2 Wash the surface.

- Prepare the cleaning solution with an approved cleaner.
- Wash the surface with the correct cleaning tool, such as a cloth towel.

3 Rinse the surface.

- Use clean water.
- Rinse the surface with the correct cleaning tool, such as a cloth towel.

4 Sanitize the surface.

- Use the correct sanitizing solution.
- Prepare the concentration per manufacturer requirements.
- Use the correct tool, such as a cloth towel, to sanitize the surface.
- Make sure the entire surface has come in contact with the sanitizing solution.

5 Allow the surface to air-dry.

When to clean and sanitize   All food-contact surfaces need to be cleaned and sanitized at these times.

- After they are used
- Before food handlers start working with a different type of food
- Any time food handlers are interrupted during a task and the items being used may have been contaminated
- After four hours if items are in constant use

Cleaning and Sanitizing Stationary Equipment

Equipment manufacturers will usually provide instructions for cleaning and sanitizing stationary equipment, such as a slicer. In general, follow these steps.

- Unplug the equipment.
- Take the removable parts off the equipment. Wash, rinse, and sanitize them by hand. You can also run the parts through a dishwasher if allowed.
- Scrape or remove food from the equipment surfaces.
- Wash the equipment surfaces. Use a cleaning solution prepared with an approved cleaner. Wash the equipment with the correct cleaning tool, such as a nylon brush or pad, or a cloth towel.
- Rinse the equipment surfaces with clean water. Use a cloth towel or other correct tool.
- Sanitize the equipment surfaces as the food handler in the photo at left is doing. Make sure the sanitizer comes in contact with each surface. The concentration of the sanitizer must meet requirements.
- Allow all surfaces to air-dry. Put the unit back together.

Clean-in-Place Equipment

Some pieces of equipment, such as soft-serve yogurt machines, are designed to have cleaning and sanitizing solutions pumped through them. Since many of them hold and dispense TCS food, they must be cleaned and sanitized every day unless otherwise indicated by the manufacturer. You should also check your local regulatory requirements.

Apply Your Knowledge

Was It Sanitized?

Circle the correct answer for each question. For all situations, assume water hardness and pH are at the correct level.

① Lee mixed a quats sanitizer with 75°F (24°C) water. A test kit showed the concentration was correct according to the manufacturer's recommendations. He soaked some utensils in the solution for 30 seconds. Were the utensils sanitized correctly?   Yes   No

② Josh mixed a chlorine sanitizer with 75°F (24°C) water. A test kit showed the concentration was 25 ppm. He soaked some tableware in the solution for 7 seconds. Was the tableware sanitized correctly?   Yes   No

③ Cecelia mixed an iodine sanitizer with 68°F (20°C) water. A test kit showed the concentration was 8 ppm. She put a pan in the solution for 30 seconds. Was the pan sanitized correctly?   Yes   No

④ Jarmin mixed a chlorine sanitizer with 100°F (38°C) water. A test kit showed the concentration was 50 ppm. She put a bowl in the solution for 7 seconds. Was the bowl sanitized correctly?   Yes   No

Take the Correct Steps

Put the steps for cleaning and sanitizing in order by writing the number of the step in the space provided.

Ⓐ _____ Sanitize the surface.

Ⓑ _____ Clean the surface.

Ⓒ _____ Allow the surface to air-dry.

Ⓓ _____ Rinse the surface.

Ⓔ _____ Remove food from the surface.

To Sanitize or Not to Sanitize

Write an ✘ next to each situation that requires the food handler to clean and sanitize the item being used.

① _____ Jorge has used the same knife to shuck oysters for 2 hours.

② _____ Bill finishes deboning chicken and wants to use the same cutting board to fillet fish.

③ _____ Mary returns to the slicer to continue slicing ham after being called away to help with the lunch rush.

④ _____ Maria has been slicing cheese on the same slicer from 8:00 a.m. to 12:00 p.m.

For answers, please turn to page 10.21.

Cleaning and Sanitizing	Dishwashing	Cleaning and Sanitizing in the Operation
— Cleaners — Sanitizers — How and When to Clean and Sanitize	— Machine Dishwashing — Manual Dishwashing — Storing Tableware and Equipment	— Cleaning the Premises — Cleaning Tools and Supplies — Developing a Cleaning Program

Dishwashing

Tableware and utensils are often cleaned and sanitized in a dishwashing machine. Larger items such as pots and pans are often cleaned by hand in a three-compartment sink. Whichever method you use, you must follow specific practices so items are cleaned and sanitized. Then you must make sure you store the items so they do not become contaminated.

Machine Dishwashing

Dishwashing machines sanitize by using either hot water or a chemical sanitizing solution.

High-Temperature Machines

High-temperature machines use hot water to clean and sanitize. If the water is not hot enough, items will not be sanitized. Extremely hot water can also bake food onto the items.

The temperature of the final sanitizing rinse must be at least 180°F (82°C), as shown in the photo at left. For stationary rack, single-temperature machines, it must be at least 165°F (74°C). The dishwasher must have a built-in thermometer that checks water temperature at the manifold, as shown in the photo at left. This is where the water sprays into the tank.

Chemical-Sanitizing Machines

Chemical-sanitizing machines can clean and sanitize items at much lower temperatures. Follow the dishwasher manufacturer's guidelines.

Dishwasher Operation

Operate your dishwasher according to the manufacturer's recommendations, and keep it in good repair. However, no matter what type of machine you use, you should follow these guidelines.

Keeping the machine clean   Clean the machine as often as needed, checking it at least once a day. Clear spray nozzles of food and foreign objects. Remove mineral deposits when needed. Fill tanks with clean water, and make sure detergent and sanitizer dispensers are filled.

Preparing items for cleaning   Scrape, rinse, or soak items before washing. Presoak items with dried-on food.

Loading dish racks   Use the correct dish racks. Load them so the water spray will reach all surfaces, as shown in the photo at left. Never overload dish racks.

Drying items   Air-dry all items. Never use a towel to dry items. You could recontaminate them.

Monitoring   Check water temperature, pressure, and sanitizer levels. Take appropriate corrective action if necessary. Operations using high-temperature dishwashing machines must provide staff with an easy and quick way to measure surface temperatures of items being sanitized. The method used must provide an irreversible record of the highest temperature reached during the sanitizing rinse. This ensures that the dishwasher can reach correct sanitizing temperatures during operation. Maximum registering thermometers or heat sensitive tape are good tools for checking temperatures.

Manual Dishwashing

Operations often use a three-compartment sink to clean and sanitize large items. The sink must be set up correctly before use, as shown in the photo at left.

- Clean and sanitize each sink and drain board.

- Fill the first sink with detergent and water. The water temperature must be at least 110°F (43°C). Follow manufacturer's recommendations.

- Fill the second sink with clean water. This is not necessary if items will be spray-rinsed instead of being dipped.

- Fill the third sink with water and sanitizer to the correct concentration. Hot water can be used as an alternative. Follow the guidelines on pages 10.2 through 10.3 and manufacturer's recommendations.

- Provide a clock with a second hand. This will let food handlers time how long items have been in the sanitizer.

How to Clean and Sanitize in a Three-Compartment Sink

Follow these steps to clean and sanitize items in a three-compartment sink.

❶ Rinse, scrape, or soak items before washing them.

If items are being soaked in the first sink, change the solution when food bits start to build up or the suds are gone.

❷ Wash items in the first sink.

Use a brush, cloth towel, or nylon scrub pad to loosen dirt. Change the water and detergent when the suds are gone or the water is dirty.

❸ Rinse items in the second sink.

Spray the items with water or dip them in it. Make sure to remove all traces of food and detergent from the items being rinsed. If dipping the items, change the rinse water when it becomes dirty or full of suds.

❹ Sanitize items in the third sink.

Change the sanitizing solution when the temperature of the water or the sanitizer concentration falls below requirements. **NEVER** rinse items after sanitizing them. This could contaminate their surfaces. The only exception to this rule is when you are washing items in a dishwasher that can safely rinse items after they have been sanitized.

❺ Air-dry items on a clean and sanitized surface.

Place items upside down so they will drain.

Pathogen Alert

Storing Tableware and Equipment

Once utensils, tableware, and equipment have been cleaned and sanitized, they must be stored in a way that will protect them from contamination. Follow these guidelines.

Storage   Store tableware and utensils at least six inches (15 centimeters) off the floor. Protect them from dirt and moisture.

Storage surfaces   Clean and sanitize drawers and shelves before storing clean items.

Glasses and flatware   Store glasses and cups upside down on a clean and sanitized shelf or rack. Store flatware and utensils with handles up, as shown in the photo at left. Staff can then pick them up without touching food-contact surfaces, which will help prevent the transfer of pathogens such as Norovirus.

Trays and carts   Clean and sanitize trays and carts used to carry clean tableware and utensils. Check them daily, and clean as often as needed.

Stationary equipment   Keep the food-contact surfaces of stationary equipment covered until ready for use.

Apply Your Knowledge

The New Dishwasher

On a separate sheet of paper, list the missing or wrong steps in the story below.

Evan started work just as the breakfast rush had begun. A load of dirty dishes had just been put into the new dishwasher. There already were a lot of pots and pans to wash in the three-compartment sink, so Evan quickly got started. He scraped the dishes into a garbage container and stacked them on the drain board next to the first sink compartment. Then he filled the first compartment with hot water and added dish detergent. He put several pans in the soapy water to soak.

Next, Evan filled the remaining two compartments with warm water. He added iodine sanitizer to the third compartment. He used a thermometer to check the water temperature and then a test kit to check the sanitizer concentration. Both were good.

Using a nylon scrub pad, Evan worked on the pans until they were clean. As he finished each one, he dipped it in the sanitizing solution. Since customers had complained of an iodine flavor on tableware, he wanted to make sure there was no sanitizer left on the pans. As he pulled each pan out of the sanitizer, he placed it into the rinse water to soak for a few seconds. Then he put it on the clean drain board to air-dry.

What did Evan do wrong?

_____

_____

_____

_____

For answers, please turn to page 10.21.

Apply Your Knowledge

Mary's Dilemma

Mary noticed that the dirty dishes had started to pile up. She quickly unloaded the dishwashing machine and got a dish cart. Mary saw a few crumbs on the cart. To clean it, she dipped a cloth towel in the dishwater in her three-compartment sink and wiped off the crumbs.

In the meantime, the carts of dirty dishes had grown. Mary quickly loaded a dish rack with as many dishes as she could fit into it. She glanced into the dishwasher before pushing in the rack. She noticed a heavy buildup of mineral deposits on the spray arm and inside the compartment. She closed the door and started the load.

What did Mary do wrong?

_____

_____

_____

_____

_____

What's Wrong with This Picture?

There are several things wrong with this three-compartment sink. Identify as many as you can in the space provided.

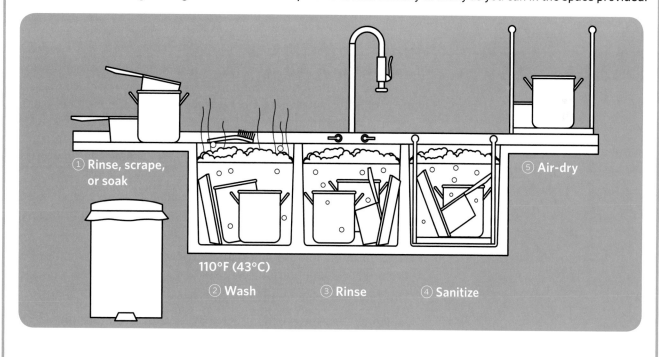

① Rinse, scrape, or soak

⑤ Air-dry

110°F (43°C)

② Wash   ③ Rinse   ④ Sanitize

_____

_____

_____

_____

_____

For answers, please turn to page 10.21.

Cleaning and Sanitizing	Dishwashing	Cleaning and Sanitizing in the Operation
— Cleaners — Sanitizers — How and When to Clean and Sanitize	— Machine Dishwashing — Manual Dishwashing — Storing Tableware and Equipment	— Cleaning the Premises — Cleaning Tools and Supplies — Developing a Cleaning Program

Cleaning and Sanitizing in the Operation

Keeping your operation clean means using the correct tools, supplies, and storage to prevent contamination. Many of the chemicals you will use are hazardous, so you also have to know how to handle them to prevent injury.

For all of your cleaning efforts to come together, you need a master cleaning schedule. Making this schedule work also means training and monitoring your staff to be sure they can follow it.

Cleaning the Premises

Nonfood-contact surfaces must be cleaned regularly. Examples include floors, ceilings, equipment exteriors, restrooms, and walls, as shown in the photo at left. Regular cleaning prevents dust, dirt, and food residue from building up.

Cleaning Up After People Who Get Sick

If a person has diarrhea or vomits in the operation, these spills must be cleaned up correctly. Vomit and diarrhea can carry Norovirus, which is highly contagious. Correct cleanup can prevent food from becoming contaminated. It will also keep others from getting sick. Check with your local regulatory authority regarding requirements for cleaning up vomit and diarrhea. In many jurisdictions, a written cleanup plan may be required.

The way you clean up vomit and diarrhea is different from the way you clean other items in the operation. There are several things to think about when developing a plan for cleaning these substances.

* How you will contain liquid and airborne substances, and remove them from the operation

* How you will clean, sanitize, and disinfect surfaces

* When to throw away food that may have been contaminated

* What equipment is needed to clean up these substances, and how it will be cleaned and disinfected after use

* When a food handler must wear personal protective equipment

* How staff will be notified of the correct procedures for containing, cleaning, and disinfecting these substances

* How to segregate contaminated areas from other areas

* When staff must be restricted from working with or around food or excluded from working in the operation

* How sick customers will be quickly removed from the operation

* How the cleaning plan will be implemented

Cleaning Tools and Supplies

Your staff needs many tools and supplies to keep the operation clean. However, these items can contaminate food and surfaces if they are not used and stored correctly.

Storing Cleaning Tools and Supplies

Cleaning tools and chemicals must be stored in a separate area away from food and prep areas. The storage area should have the following.

- Good lighting so staff can see chemicals easily
- Hooks for hanging mops, brooms, and other cleaning tools
- Utility sink for filling buckets and washing cleaning tools
- Floor drain for dumping dirty water, as shown in the photo at left

To prevent contamination, NEVER clean mops, brushes, or other tools in sinks used for handwashing, food prep, or dishwashing. Additionally, NEVER dump mop water or other liquid waste into toilets or urinals.

When storing cleaning tools, consider the following.

- Air-dry towels overnight.
- Hang mops, brooms, and brushes on hooks to air-dry.
- Clean and rinse buckets. Let them air-dry, and then store them with other tools.

Using Foodservice Chemicals

Many of the chemicals used in the operation can be hazardous, especially if they are used the wrong way. To reduce your risk, you should only use chemicals that are approved for use in a foodservice operation. You should also follow these guidelines.

Storage and labeling   Store chemicals in their original containers away from food and prep areas, as shown in the photo at left. Separate by spacing or partitioning. If chemicals are transferred to a new container, the label on that container must list the common name of the chemical.

Disposal   When throwing out chemicals, follow the instructions on the label and any requirements from your local regulatory authority.

Material Safety Data Sheets   The Occupational Safety and Health Administration (OSHA) has requirements for using chemicals. OSHA requires chemical manufacturers and suppliers to provide a Material Safety Data Sheet (MSDS) for each hazardous chemical they sell. An MSDS contains the following information about the chemical.

* Safe use and handling

* Physical, health, fire, and reactivity hazards

* Precautions

* Appropriate personal protective equipment (PPE) to wear when using the chemical

* First-aid information and steps to take in an emergency

* Manufacturer's name, address, and phone number

* Preparation date of MSDS

* Hazardous ingredients and identity information

MSDS are often sent with the chemical shipment. You can also request them from your supplier or the manufacturer. Staff have a right to see an MSDS for any hazardous chemical they work with. Therefore, you must keep these sheets where they can be accessed. The photo at left shows how one operation makes them available to staff.

Developing a Cleaning Program

To develop an effective cleaning program for your operation, you must focus on three things.

❶ Creating a master cleaning schedule

❷ Training your staff to follow it

❸ Monitoring the program to make sure it works

Creating a Master Cleaning Schedule

Create a master cleaning schedule with the following information.

What should be cleaned   List all cleaning jobs in one area. Or list jobs in the order they should be performed.

Who should clean it   Assign each task to a specific individual.

When it should be cleaned   Staff should clean and sanitize as needed. Schedule major cleaning when food will not be contaminated or service will not be affected. Schedule work shifts to allow enough time.

How it should be cleaned   Have clear, written procedures for cleaning. List cleaning tools and chemicals by name. Post cleaning instructions near the item, as shown in the photo at left. Always follow manufacturers' instructions when cleaning equipment.

Training Your Staff to Follow the Program

Schedule time for training. Work with small groups or conduct training by area.

Monitoring the Cleaning Program

Make sure the cleaning program is working.

- Supervise daily cleaning routines.

- Check all cleaning tasks against the master schedule every day.

- Change the master schedule as needed for any changes in menu, procedures, or equipment.

- Ask staff during meetings for input on the program.

Apply Your Knowledge

Is It Stored Correctly?

Write an ✗ next to the situation if the food handler stored the cleaning tool or material the correct way.

①_____ Sheryl received a shipment of cleaning supplies. Along with the invoice, the supplier gave her an MSDS for the new brand of cleaner she ordered. She filed the MSDS with the invoice in a locked cabinet.

②_____ Raul noticed that a bottle of chemical cleaner in the storage area was leaking. Fortunately, there was a nearly empty spray bottle of the same cleaner, so he poured the remainder into it. The label on the spray bottle listed the common name of the chemical.

③_____ Sasha emptied a bucket of dirty mop water into the floor drain in the chemical-storage room. He rinsed the mop and hung it to dry. Then he cleaned and rinsed the bucket.

④_____ Laura washed and rinsed a prep table. Then she sanitized the table by spraying it with sanitizer and allowed it to air-dry. When she was finished, she placed the bottle of sanitizer on the prep table so it would be there the next time she needed it.

⑤_____ Maurice used a cleaner on the dishwasher. The sprayer on the bottle stopped working when it was only half empty, so he threw it in the garbage.

What's Wrong with This Picture?

There are many things wrong with this storage area. Identify as many as you can in the space provided.

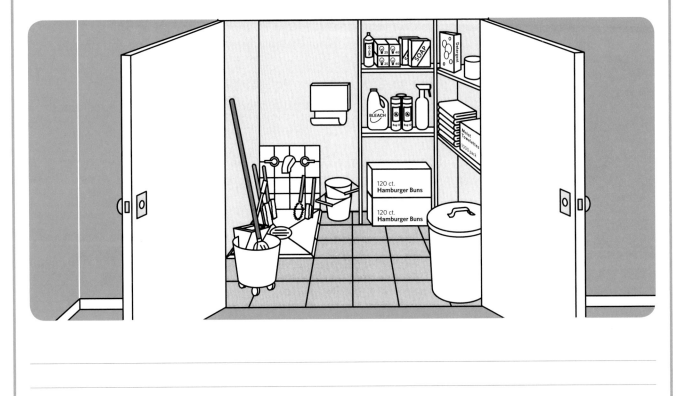

_____

_____

_____

_____

_____

For answers, please turn to page 10.22.

Chapter Summary

- Cleaning removes food and other dirt from a surface. Sanitizing reduces the number of harmful pathogens on a surface to safe levels. You must clean and rinse a surface before it can be sanitized. Then the surface must be allowed to air-dry. Surfaces can be sanitized with hot water or a chemical-sanitizing solution.

- All surfaces should be cleaned and rinsed. Food-contact surfaces must be cleaned and sanitized after every use. You should also clean and sanitize each time you begin working with a different type of food or when a task is interrupted. If items are in constant use, they must be cleaned and sanitized every four hours.

- Tableware and utensils can be washed in dishwashers or by hand in a three-compartment sink. Always follow manufacturers' instructions when using dishwashers. Make sure your machine is clean and in good working condition. Check the temperature and pressure of wash-and-rinse cycles daily.

- Three-compartment sinks and drain boards must be cleaned and sanitized before they are used for dish washing. Items washed in a three-compartment sink should be rinsed or scraped clean before washing. They should then be washed in a detergent solution and rinsed in clean water. Next, they should be sanitized in either hot water or in a chemical-sanitizing solution for a specific amount of time. Finally, they should be air-dried. Once cleaned and sanitized, tableware and equipment should be protected from contamination.

- Make sure chemicals are clearly labeled. Keep MSDS for each chemical in a location accessible to all staff while on the job.

- Create a master cleaning schedule listing all cleaning tasks. Monitor the cleaning program to keep it effective and supervise cleaning procedures. Make adjustments as needed.

Chapter Review Case Study

Keeping a clean and sanitized operation involves using the correct tools and products for a cleaning job; cleaning and sanitizing items the correct way at the right time; storing items so they remain safe to use; handling chemicals the correct way; and developing and following a cleaning program.

Now, take what you have learned in this chapter and apply it to the following case study.

Tom was just hired as the new general manager at the Twin Trees Family Restaurant. One of his first projects was to create a new cleaning program. He started by taking a walk through the operation. His first stop was the storage area for cleaning tools and supplies. It had a utility sink and a floor drain, but the hot water in the sink wasn't working. He also noticed two sets of mops and brooms stored on the floor. The storage area was small, but it was well organized and well lit. All the containers were clearly labeled.

① Should Tom suggest any changes to the storage room, tools, or chemicals?

Yes _____ No _____ If yes, what changes should he suggest?

_____

_____

Next, Tom watched Clara, a new prep cook, to see how she cleaned and sanitized her areas. Clara cut some melons on a cutting board. Then she wiped it down with a cloth towel. Clara put the cloth towel in a bucket of sanitizing solution to soak while she butterflied some pork chops on the board. Using the same cloth towel, she wiped down the board after she finished the pork chops. Then, she chopped some onions and sautéed them in a large stock pot. While the onions were sautéing, Clara wiped the board a third time with the same cloth towel.

② Did Clara do anything wrong?

Yes _____ No _____ If yes, what changes should he suggest?

_____

_____

Tom also watched many other staff members perform cleaning and sanitizing tasks that week. With the help of some senior staff, Tom created a master cleaning schedule.

③ What steps should Tom take to make sure everyone follows the master cleaning schedule?

_____

_____

For answers, please turn to page 10.22.

Study Questions

Circle the best answer to each question.

① **What is required for measuring the sanitizing rinse temperature in a high-temperature dishwashing machine?**

  A Infrared thermometer

  B Time-temperature indicator

  C Maximum registering thermometer

  D Thermocouple with immersion probe

② **What is sanitizing?**

  A Reducing dirt from a surface

  B Reducing the pH of a surface

  C Reducing the hardness of water

  D Reducing pathogens to safe levels

③ **If food-contact surfaces are in constant use, how often must they be cleaned and sanitized?**

  A Every 4 hours

  B Every 5 hours

  C Every 6 hours

  D Every 7 hours

④ **What must food handlers do to make sure sanitizing solution for use on food-contact surfaces has been made correctly?**

  A Test the solution with a sanitizer kit.

  B Use very hot water when making the solution.

  C Try out the solution on a food-contact surface.

  D Mix the solution with equal parts of water.

⑤ **A food handler was assigned to clean a slicer that was too difficult to move. The slicer was unplugged. Then the removable parts were taken off the slicer and cleaned and sanitized in a three-compartment sink. Food bits on the slicer were removed. After the machine was wiped down with detergent and water, it was sanitized and allowed to air-dry. Then the food handler put the machine back together. What mistake did the food handler make?**

  A Failed to dry the machine with a clean cloth after sanitizing it

  B Failed to sanitize the machine before taking the removable parts off

  C Failed to rinse the machine after wiping it down with detergent and water

  D Failed to wash the machine with detergent and water before taking it apart

Continued on the next page ▶

▶ *Continued from previous page*

⑥ **What should be done when throwing away chemicals?**

A Seal the container and recycle it.

B Seal the container in a bag and place it in the garbage.

C Follow label instructions and regulatory requirements.

D Pour leftover chemicals into a drain and throw the container away.

⑦ **How should flatware and utensils that have been cleaned and sanitized be stored?**

A With handles facing up

B Below cleaning supplies

C In drawers that have been washed and rinsed

D Four inches (10 centimeters) from the floor

⑧ **What is the correct way to clean and sanitize a prep table?**

A Remove food from the surface, wash, rinse, sanitize, air-dry

B Remove food from the surface, sanitize, rinse, wash, air-dry

C Remove food from the surface, wash, sanitize, air-dry, rinse

D Remove food from the surface, air-dry, wash, rinse, sanitize

For answers, please turn to page 10.22.

Answers

10.6 Was It Sanitized?

① Yes

② No

③ No

④ Yes

10.6 Take the Correct Steps

4, 2, 5, 3, 1

10.6 To Sanitize or Not to Sanitize

2, 3, and 4 should be marked.

10.10 The New Dishwasher

Here is what Evan did wrong.

- He did not clean and sanitize the sink compartments and drain boards before starting.

- He did not check the water temperature in the first sink compartment.

- He did not rinse the items before sanitizing them. He rinsed the items after sanitizing, which could contaminate them.

- He did not time how long the pots and pans were in the sanitizer.

10.11 Mary's Dilemma

Here is what Mary did wrong.

- She did not clean and sanitize the cart for clean tableware.

- She did not rinse, scrape, or soak the dirty dishes before putting them into the dish rack.

- She overloaded the dish rack.

- She did not clean the heavy mineral deposits from the machine before starting the day.

10.11 What's Wrong with This Picture?

① There is no clock with a second hand. Staff would not be able to time how long an item has been immersed in the sanitizer.

② Soap suds from the wash compartment have been carried over into the rinse compartment and the sanitizer compartment. This can deplete the sanitizer.

③ A cleaned and sanitized pot is not being air-dried correctly. It should be upside down.

Continued on the next page ▶

▶ *Continued from previous page*

10.16   Is It Stored Correctly?

2 and 3 should be marked.

10.16   What's Wrong with This Picture?

① There are no hooks for the brushes and mop to air-dry.

② The chemical spray bottle is not labeled.

③ Food is being stored in the area.

10.18   Chapter Review Case Study

① Tom should have the hot water fixed. He also should have hooks installed to hang up the mops and brooms.

② Clara should have washed, rinsed, and sanitized the cutting board at these times.

- Before cutting the melons
- After cutting melons and before butterflying pork chops
- After butterflying pork chops and before chopping onions
- After chopping onions

③ For Tom's cleaning program to work, he should do the following.

- Train the staff on the cleaning and sanitizing tasks.
- Supervise daily cleaning routines.
- Check all cleaning tasks against the master cleaning schedule daily.
- Ask staff during meetings for input on the program.

10.19   Study Questions

① C

② D

③ A

④ A

⑤ C

⑥ C

⑦ A

⑧ A

Notes

Organisms That Cause Foodborne Illness

Bacteria

Bacteria	*Bacillus cereus* (ba-SIL-us SEER-ee-us)
Illness	*Bacillus cereus* gastroenteritis (ba-SIL-us SEER-ee-us GAS-tro-EN-ter-I-tiss)

Bacillus cereus is a spore-forming bacteria found in dirt. It can produce two different toxins when allowed to grow to high levels. The toxins cause different illnesses.

Food Commonly Linked with the Bacteria	Most Common Symptoms	Prevention Measures
Diarrhea illness	Diarrhea illness	• Cook food to minimum internal temperatures.
• Cooked vegetables	• Watery diarrhea	• Hold food at the correct temperatures.
• Meat products	• No vomiting	• Cool food correctly.
• Milk	Vomiting illness	• Control time and temperature.
Vomiting illness	• Nausea	
• Cooked rice dishes, including fried rice and rice pudding	• Vomiting	

Bacteria	*Listeria monocytogenes* (liss-TEER-ee-uh MON-o-SI-TAHJ-uh-neez)
Illness	Listeriosis (liss-TEER-ee-O-sis)

Listeria monocytogenes is found in dirt, water, and plants. Unlike other bacteria, it grows in cool, moist environments. The illness is uncommon in healthy people, but high-risk populations are especially vulnerable—particularly pregnant women.

Food Commonly Linked with the Bacteria	Most Common Symptoms	Prevention Measures
• Raw meat	Pregnant women	• Throw out any product that has passed its use-by or expiration date.
• Unpasteurized dairy products	• Miscarriage	• Cook raw meat to minimum internal temperatures.
• Ready-to-eat food, such as deli meat, hot dogs, and soft cheeses	Newborns	• Prevent cross-contamination between raw or undercooked food and ready-to-eat food.
	• Sepsis	• Avoid using unpasteurized dairy products.
	• Pneumonia	• Control time and temperature.
	• Meningitis	

Bacteria	Shiga toxin-producing *Escherichia coli* (ess-chur-EE-kee-UH KO-LI)**(STEC)**, also known as *E. coli*. It includes O157:H7, O26:H7, O26:H11, O111:H8, and O158:NM
Illness	Hemorrhagic colitis (hem-or-RA-jik ko-LI-tiss)

Shiga toxin-producing *E. coli* can be found in the intestines of cattle. It is also found in infected people. The bacteria can contaminate meat during slaughtering. Eating only a small amount of the bacteria can make a person sick. Once eaten, it produces toxins in the intestines, which causes the illness. The bacteria are often in a person's feces for weeks after symptoms have ended.

Food Commonly Linked with the Bacteria	Most Common Symptoms	Prevention Measures
• Ground beef (raw and undercooked) • Contaminated produce	• Diarrhea (eventually becomes bloody) • Abdominal cramps • Kidney failure (in severe cases)	• Cook food, especially ground beef, to minimum internal temperatures. • Purchase produce from approved, reputable suppliers. • Prevent cross-contamination between raw meat and ready-to-eat food. • Keep staff with diarrhea out of the operation. • Keep staff who have diarrhea and have been diagnosed with hemorrhagic colitis out of the operation. • Control time and temperature.

Bacteria	*Clostridium perfringens*
Illness	*Clostridium perfringens* gastroenteritis (klos-TRID-ee-um per-FRIN-jins GAS-tro-EN-ter-I-tiss)

Clostridium perfringens is found in dirt, where it forms spores that allow it to survive. It is also carried in the intestines of both animals and humans.

Clostridium perfringens does not grow at refrigeration temperatures. It does grow rapidly in food in the temperature danger zone. Commercially prepped food is not often involved in outbreaks. People who get sick usually do not have nausea, fever, or vomiting.

Food Commonly Linked with the Bacteria	Most Common Symptoms	Prevention Measures
• Meat • Poultry • Dishes made with meat and poultry, such as stews and gravies	• Diarrhea • Severe abdominal pain	• Cool and reheat food correctly. • Hold food at the correct temperatures. • Control time and temperature.

Bacteria   *Clostridium botulinum* (klos-TRID-ee-um BOT-chew-LINE-um)

Illness   Botulism (BOT-chew-liz-um)

Clostridium botulinum forms spores that are often found in water and dirt. These spores can contaminate almost any food. The bacteria do not grow well in refrigerated or highly acidic food or in food with low moisture. However, *Clostridium botulinum* grows without oxygen and can produce a lethal toxin when food is time-temperature abused. Without medical treatment, death is likely.

Food Commonly Linked with the Bacteria	Most Common Symptoms	Prevention Measures
• Incorrectly canned food	Initially	• Hold, cool, and reheat food correctly.
• Reduced-oxygen packaged (ROP) food	• Nausea and vomiting	• Inspect canned food for damage.
• Temperature-abused vegetables, such as baked potatoes	Later	• Control time and temperature.
	• Weakness	
• Untreated garlic-and-oil mixtures	• Double vision	
	• Difficulty in speaking and swallowing	

Bacteria   *Campylobacter jejuni* (Camp-ee-lo-BAK-ter jay-JUNE-ee)

Illness   Campylobacteriosis (CAMP-ee-lo-BAK-teer-ee-O-sis)

Though *Campylobacter jejuni* is commonly associated with poultry, it has been known to contaminate water. Illness often occurs when poultry is incorrectly cooked and when raw poultry has been allowed to cross-contaminate other food and food-contact surfaces. Campylobacteriosis is best controlled through correct cooking and the prevention of cross-contamination.

Food Commonly Linked with the Bacteria	Most Common Symptoms	Prevention Measures
• Poultry	• Diarrhea (may be watery or bloody)	• Cook food, particularly poultry, to required minimum internal temperatures.
• Water contaminated with the bacteria	• Abdominal cramps	
• Meats	• Fever	• Prevent cross-contamination between raw poultry and ready-to-eat food.
• Stews/gravies	• Vomiting	
	• Headaches	• Control time and temperature.

Bacteria   Nontyphoidal *Salmonella* (SAL-me-NEL-uh)

Illness   Salmonellosis (SAL-men-uh-LO-sis)

Many farm animals carry nontyphoidal *Salmonella* naturally. Eating only a small amount of these bacteria can make a person sick. How severe symptoms are depends on the health of the person and the amount of bacteria eaten. The bacteria are often in a person's feces for weeks after symptoms have ended.

Food Commonly Linked with the Bacteria	Most Common Symptoms	Prevention Measures
• Poultry and eggs	• Diarrhea	• Cook poultry and eggs to minimum internal temperatures.
• Meat	• Abdominal cramps	• Prevent cross-contamination between poultry and ready-to-eat food.
• Milk and dairy products	• Vomiting	• Keep food handlers who are vomiting or have diarrhea and have been diagnosed with an illness from nontyphoidal *Salmonella* out of the operation.
• Produce, such as tomatoes, peppers, and cantaloupes	• Fever	

Bacteria   *Salmonella* Typhi (SAL-me-NEL-uh Ti-fee)

Illness   Typhoid fever

Salmonella Typhi lives only in humans. People with typhoid fever carry the bacteria in their bloodstream and intestinal tract. Eating only a small amount of these bacteria can make a person sick. The severity of symptoms depends on the health of the person and the amount of bacteria eaten. The bacteria are often in a person's feces for weeks after symptoms have ended.

Food Commonly Linked with the Bacteria	Most Common Symptoms	Prevention Measures
• Ready-to-eat food	• High fever	• Exclude food handlers who have been diagnosed with an illness caused by *Salmonella* Typhi from the operation.
• Beverages	• Weakness	• Wash hands.
	• Abdominal pain	• Cook food to minimum internal temperatures.
	• Headache	• Prevent cross-contamination.
	• Loss of appetite	
	• Rash	

Bacteria   *Shigella* **spp.** *(shi-GEL-uh)*

Illness   Shigellosis *(SHIG-uh-LO-sis)*

Shigella spp. is found in the feces of humans with the illness. Most illnesses occur when people eat or drink contaminated food or water. Flies can also transfer the bacteria from feces to food. Eating only a small amount of these bacteria can make a person sick. High levels of the bacteria are often in a person's feces for weeks after symptoms have ended.

Food Commonly Linked with the Bacteria	Most Common Symptoms	Prevention Measures
• Food that is easily contaminated by hands, such as salads containing TCS food (potato, tuna, shrimp, macaroni, and chicken) • Food that has made contact with contaminated water, such as produce	• Bloody diarrhea • Abdominal pain and cramps • Fever (occasionally)	• Exclude food handlers who have diarrhea and have been diagnosed with an illness caused by *Shigella* spp. from the operation. • Wash hands. • Control flies inside and outside the operation. • Practice personal hygiene.

Bacteria   *Staphylococcus aureus* *(STAF-uh-lo-KOK-us OR-ee-us)*

Illness   Staphylococcal gastroenteritis *(STAF-ul-lo-KOK-al GAS-tro-EN-ter-I-tiss)*

Staphylococcus aureus can be found in humans—particularly in the hair, nose, and throat; and in infected cuts. It is often transferred to food when people carrying it touch these areas on their bodies and then handle food without washing their hands. If allowed to grow to large numbers in food, the bacteria can produce toxins that cause the illness when eaten. Cooking cannot destroy these toxins, so preventing bacterial growth is critical.

Food Commonly Linked with the Bacteria	Most Common Symptoms	Prevention Measures
• Food that requires handling during prepping • Salads containing TCS food (egg, tuna, chicken, and macaroni) • Deli meat	• Nausea • Vomiting and retching • Abdominal cramps	• Wash hands, particularly after touching the hair, face, or body. • Cover wounds on hands and arms. • Hold, cool, and reheat food correctly. • Practice personal hygiene.

Bacteria   *Vibrio vulnificus* **and** *Vibrio parahaemolyticus* *(VIB-ree-o vul-NIF-ih-kus and VIB-ree-o PAIR-uh-HEE-mo-lit-ih-kus)*

Illnesses   *Vibrio* gastroenteritis *(VIB-ree-o GAS-tro-EN-ter-I-tiss)*

            Vibrio vulnificus primary septicemia *(VIB-ree-o vul-NIF-ih-kus SEP-ti-SEE-mee-uh)*

These bacteria are found in the waters where shellfish are harvested. They can grow very rapidly at temperatures in the middle of the temperature danger zone. People with chronic conditions (such as diabetes or cirrhosis) who become sick from these bacteria may get primary septicemia. This severe illness can lead to death.

Food Commonly Linked with the Bacteria	Most Common Symptoms	Prevention Measures
• Oysters from contaminated water	• Diarrhea • Abdominal cramps and nausea • Vomiting • Low-grade fever and chills	• Cook oysters to minimum internal temperatures. • Purchase from approved, reputable suppliers.

Viruses

Virus   Hepatitis A *(HEP-a-TI-tiss)*

Illness   Hepatitis A

Hepatitis A is mainly found in the feces of people infected with it. The virus can contaminate water and many types of food. It is commonly linked with ready-to-eat food. However, it has also been linked with shellfish from contaminated water.

The virus is often transferred to food when infected food handlers touch food or equipment with fingers that have feces on them. Eating only a small amount of the virus can make a person sick. An infected person may not show symptoms for weeks but can be very infectious. Cooking does not destroy hepatitis A.

Food Commonly Linked with the Virus
- Ready-to-eat food
- Shellfish from contaminated water

Most Common Symptoms
- Fever (mild)
- General weakness
- Nausea
- Abdominal pain
- Jaundice (appears later)

Prevention Measures
- Exclude staff who have been diagnosed with hepatitis A from the operation.
- Exclude staff who have jaundice from the operation.
- Wash hands.
- Avoid bare-hand contact with ready-to-eat food.
- Purchase shellfish from approved, reputable suppliers.
- Practice personal hygiene.

Virus   Norovirus *(NOR-o-VI-rus)*

Illness   Norovirus gastroenteritis

Like hepatitis A, Norovirus is commonly linked with ready-to-eat food. It has also been linked with contaminated water. Norovirus is often transferred to food when infected food handlers touch food or equipment with fingers that have feces on them.

Eating only a small amount of Norovirus can make a person sick. It is also very contagious. People become contagious within a few hours after eating it. The virus is often in a person's feces for days after symptoms have ended.

Food Commonly Linked with the Virus
- Ready-to-eat food
- Shellfish from contaminated water

Most Common Symptoms
- Vomiting
- Diarrhea
- Nausea
- Abdominal cramps

Prevention Measures
- Exclude staff who are vomiting or have diarrhea and have been diagnosed with Norovirus from the operation.
- Wash hands.
- Avoid bare-hand contact with ready-to-eat food.
- Purchase shellfish from approved, reputable suppliers.
- Practice personal hygiene.

Parasites

Parasite   *Anisakis* simplex *(ANN-ih-SAHK-iss SIM-plex)*

Illness   **Anisakiasis** *(ANN-ih-SAH-KYE-ah-sis)*

People can get sick when they eat raw or undercooked fish containing this parasite.

Food Commonly Linked with the Parasite

Raw and undercooked fish

- Herring
- Cod
- Halibut
- Mackerel
- Pacific salmon

Most Common Symptoms

- Tingling in throat
- Coughing up worms

Prevention Measures

- Cook fish to minimum internal temperatures.
- If serving raw or undercooked fish, purchase sushi-grade fish that has been frozen to the correct time-temperature requirements.
- Purchase from approved, reputable suppliers.

Parasite   *Cryptosporidium parvum* *(KRIP-TOH-spor-ID-ee-um PAR-vum)*

Illness   **Cryptosporidiosis** *(KRIP-TOH-spor-id-ee-O-sis)*

Cryptosporidium parvum can be found in the feces of infected people. Food handlers can transfer it to food when they touch food with fingers that have feces on them. Day-care and medical communities have been frequent locations of person-to-person spread of this parasite. Symptoms will be more severe in people with weakened immune systems.

Food Commonly Linked with the Parasite

- Contaminated water
- Produce

Most Common Symptoms

- Watery diarrhea
- Abdominal cramps
- Nausea
- Weight loss

Prevention Measures

- Use correctly treated water.
- Keep food handlers with diarrhea out of the operation.
- Wash hands.
- Purchase from approved, reputable suppliers.

Parasite   *Giardia duodenalis* (jee-ARE-dee-uh do-WAH-den-AL-is), **also known as** *G. lamblia* **or** *G. intestinalis*

Illness   Giardiasis (JEE-are-DYE-uh-sis)

Giardia duodenalis can be found in the feces of infected people. Food handlers can transfer the parasite to food when they touch food with fingers that have feces on them.

Food Commonly Linked with the Parasite	Most Common Symptoms	Prevention Measures
• Incorrectly treated water • Produce	Initially • Fever Later • Diarrhea • Abdominal cramps • Nausea	• Use correctly treated water. • Keep food handlers with diarrhea out of the operation. • Wash hands. • Purchase from approved, reputable suppliers.

Parasite   *Cyclospora cayetanensis* (SI-klo-spor-uh KI-uh-te-NEN-sis)

Illness   Cyclosporiasis (SI-klo-spor-I-uh-sis)

Cyclospora cayetanensis is a parasite that has been found in contaminated water and has been associated with produce irrigated or washed with contaminated water. It can also be found in the feces of infected people. Food handlers can transfer the parasite to food when they touch it with fingers containing feces. For this reason, food handlers with diarrhea must be excluded from the operation. It is also critical to purchase produce from approved, reputable suppliers.

Food Commonly Linked with the Parasite	Most Common Symptoms	Prevention Measures
• Incorrectly treated water • Produce such as berries, lettuce, or basil	• Nausea • Abdominal cramps • Mild fever • Diarrhea alternating with constipation • Loss of weight • Loss of appetite	• Purchase produce from approved, reputable suppliers. • Keep food handlers with diarrhea out of the operation. • Wash hands.

Toxins

Toxin	Histamine *(HISS-ta-meen)*
Illness	Scombroid poisoning *(SKOM-broyd)*

Histamine poisoning can occur when high levels of histamine in scombroid and other species of fish are eaten. When the fish are time-temperature abused, bacteria on the fish make the toxin. It cannot be destroyed by freezing, cooking, smoking, or curing.

Food Commonly Linked with the Toxin

- Tuna
- Bonito
- Mackerel
- Mahimahi

Most Common Symptoms

Initially

- Reddening of the face and neck
- Sweating
- Headache
- Burning or tingling sensation in the mouth or throat

Possibly later

- Diarrhea
- Vomiting

Prevention Measures

- Prevent time-temperature abuse during storage and prepping.
- Purchase from approved, reputable suppliers.

Toxin	Ciguatoxin *(SIG-wa-TOX-in)*
Illness	Ciguatera fish poisoning *(SIG-wa-TAIR-uh)*

Ciguatoxin is found in some marine algae. The toxin builds up in certain fish when they eat smaller fish that have eaten the toxic algae. Ciguatoxin cannot be detected by smell or taste. It is not eliminated by cooking or freezing the fish. Symptoms may last months or years depending on how severe the illness is.

Food Commonly Linked with the Toxin

Predatory tropical reef fish from the Pacific Ocean, the western part of the Indian Ocean, and the Caribbean Sea.

- Barracuda
- Grouper
- Jacks
- Snapper

Most Common Symptoms

- Reversal of hot and cold sensations
- Nausea
- Vomiting
- Tingling in fingers, lips, or toes
- Joint and muscle pain

Prevention Measures

- Purchase predatory tropical reef fish from approved, reputable suppliers.

Toxin   Saxitoxin *(SAX-ih-TOX-in)*

Illness   **Paralytic shellfish poisoning (PSP)** *(PAIR-ah-LIT-ik)*

Some types of shellfish can become contaminated as they filter toxic algae from the water. People get sick with paralytic shellfish poisoning (PSP) when they eat these shellfish. Saxitoxin cannot be smelled or tasted. It is not destroyed by cooking or freezing. Death from paralysis may result if high levels of the toxin are eaten.

Food Commonly Linked with the Toxin	Most Common Symptoms	Prevention Measures
Shellfish found in colder waters, such as those of the Pacific and New England coasts.	• Numbness	• Purchase shellfish from approved, reputable suppliers.
• Clams	• Tingling of the mouth, face, arms, and legs	
• Mussels	• Dizziness	
• Oysters	• Nausea	
• Scallops	• Vomiting	
	• Diarrhea	

Toxin   Brevetoxin *(BREV-ih-TOX-in)*

Illness   **Neurotoxic shellfish poisoning (NSP)** *(NUR-o-TOX-ik)*

Some types of shellfish can become contaminated as they filter toxic algae from the water. People get sick with neurotoxic shellfish poisoning (NSP) when they eat these shellfish. Brevetoxin cannot be smelled or tasted. It is not destroyed by cooking or freezing.

Food Commonly Linked with the Toxin	Most Common Symptoms	Prevention Measures
Shellfish found in the warmer waters of the west coast of Florida, the Gulf of Mexico, and the Caribbean Sea.	• Tingling and numbness of the lips, tongue, and throat	• Purchase shellfish from approved, reputable suppliers.
• Clams	• Dizziness	
• Mussels	• Reversal of hot and cold sensations	
• Oysters	• Vomiting	
	• Diarrhea	

Toxin   Domoic acid *(duh-MO-ik)*

Illness   **Amnesic shellfish poisoning (ASP)** *(am-NEE-zik)*

Some types of shellfish can become contaminated as they filter toxic algae from the water. People get sick with amnesic shellfish poisoning (ASP) when they eat these shellfish. The severity of symptoms depends on the amount of toxin eaten and the health of the person. Domoic acid cannot be smelled or tasted. It is not destroyed by cooking or freezing.

Food Commonly Linked with the Toxin	Most Common Symptoms	Prevention Measures
Shellfish found in the coastal waters of the Pacific Northwest and the east coast of Canada.	Initially	• Purchase shellfish from approved, reputable suppliers.
• Clams	• Vomiting	
• Mussels	• Diarrhea	
• Oysters	• Abdominal pain	
• Scallops	Possibly later	
	• Confusion	
	• Memory loss	
	• Disorientation	
	• Seizure	
	• Coma	

Notes

Index